Hugh Thompson

Lambeth Conference, 1897:

Full report of the proceedings of the public meetings of the Society for the Propagation of the Gospel and welcome to the Bishops from foreign parts: together with the sermon preached in St. Paul's Cathedral, on Wednesday,

Hugh Thompson

Lambeth Conference, 1897:
Full report of the proceedings of the public meetings of the Society for the Propagation of the Gospel and welcome to the Bishops from foreign parts: together with the sermon preached in St. Paul's Cathedral, on Wednesday,

ISBN/EAN: 9783337713942

Printed in Europe, USA, Canada, Australia, Japan

Cover: Foto ©ninafisch / pixelio.de

More available books at **www.hansebooks.com**

ns
AMBETH CONFERENCE 1897

FULL REPORT OF THE PROCEEDINGS

OF THE

PUBLIC MEETINGS

OF THE

Society for the Propagation of the Gospel

AND

ELCOME TO THE BISHOPS FROM FOREIGN PARTS

TOGETHER WITH THE

SERMON

PREACHED IN ST PAUL'S CATHEDRAL

On Wednesday, June 23, 1897

BY THE RIGHT REV.

THE LORD BISHOP OF MISSISSIPPI, U.S.A.

LONDON
PUBLISHED BY THE
Society for the Propagation of the Gospel in Foreign Parts
19 DELAHAY STREET, S.W.
AND BY
WELLS GARDNER, DARTON & CO.
3 PATERNOSTER BUILDINGS, E.C.

Classified Digest of the **RECORDS OF THE SOCIETY FOR THE PROPAGATION OF THE GOSPEL IN FOREIGN PARTS, 1701-1892** (*with much Supplementary Information*) Every State in America, and every Colony in which the Society has worked, comes under review in its turn, and its Ecclesiastical History is given succinctly and sufficiently, with copious references to the authorities on which each statement rests. The Missionary work in India, as well as in countries outside the limits of the Empire, is recorded at length, and a record is given of all the Missionaries whom the Society has supported during the last 19 years. The book is illustrated by Portraits of fourteen Arch bishops of Canterbury who have been its presidents; of Bishop Seabury, the first Bishop of the United States; and of the Rev. G Keith, the first Missionary sent to America in 1702; and with illustrations of many Colleges in foreign parts, which the Society has helped by endowment or otherwise. *Cheap Unabridged Edition* (Fifth Edition), price 7s. 6d. (pp. 1,000, 8vo.).
Received with unanimous praise by the press in all parts of th world.

THE RAMSDEN SERMON, preached before the University of Cambridge on Whitsun Day, 1897, by the Right Rev H. B. WHIPPLE, D.D., Lord Bishop of Minnesota, U.S.A. Price 3d

CHURCH EXTENSION in the COLONIES and DEPENDENCIES. The Ramsden Sermon for 1892, preached before the University of Oxford on Trinity Sunday, June 12, 1892 by the Rev. H. W. TUCKER, M.A., Secretary of the Society for the Propagation of the Gospel in Foreign Parts, and Honorary Secretary of the Colonial Bishoprics Fund. Price 2d.

S.P.G. PICTURE BOOK. 96 pages, demy 4to., pri 3s. 6d. A Book for Children, designed to show them the continui of Missions. With Illustrations of—I. THE NEW TESTAMENT From the Pictures of old and living Masters, beginning with the visit of the "Wise Men of the East" to the Infant Saviour II. THE INTRODUCTION OF CHRISTIANITY IN ENGLAND From Original Designs. III. SCENES IN THE WORK OF TH S.P.G. With many new Pictures. Cover designed by HEYWOO SUMNER. Edited by C. E. BUNYON.

SOCIETY FOR THE PROPAGATION OF THE GOSPEL

19 DELAHAY STREET, WESTMINSTER, S.W.

LAMBETH CONFERENCE 1897

FULL REPORT OF THE PROCEEDINGS

OF THE

PUBLIC MEETINGS

OF THE

Society for the Propagation of the Gospel

AND

WELCOME TO THE BISHOPS FROM FOREIGN PARTS

TOGETHER WITH THE

SERMON

PREACHED IN ST. PAUL'S CATHEDRAL

On Wednesday, June 23, 1897

BY THE RIGHT REV.

THE LORD BISHOP OF MISSISSIPPI, U.S.A.

LONDON
PUBLISHED BY THE
Society for the Propagation of the Gospel in Foreign Parts
19 DELAHAY STREET, S.W.
AND BY
WELLS GARDNER, DARTON & CO.
3 PATERNOSTER BUILDINGS, E.C.

Price 1s. *net; by post* 1s. 1d.

PRINTED BY
SPOTTISWOODE AND CO., NEW-STREET SQUARE
LONDON

CONTENTS

	PAGE
INTRODUCTION	v
SERMON BY THE LORD BISHOP OF MISSISSIPPI	7

MORNING MEETING

ADDRESS OF WELCOME AND BRIEF REPORT	18
ADDRESS BY THE ARCHBISHOP OF YORK	20
THE EXTENSION OF THE EPISCOPATE AND CHURCH ORGANIZATION IN INDIA, by *the Most Rev. the Lord Bishop of Calcutta*	23
MISSIONS TO THE ABORIGINES OF INDIA, by *the Lord Bishop of Chhota Nagpur*	27
THE CHURCH IN JAPAN, by *the Lord Bishop of South Tokyo*	32
THE MISSION TO COREA, by *the Right Rev. Bishop Corfe*	35
THE PROVINCE OF SOUTH AFRICA, by *the Most Reverend the Lord Bishop of Cape Town*	39
THE CHURCH'S WORK AMONG THE NATIVE TRIBES OF SOUTH AFRICA, by *the Lord Bishop of St. John's*	43
THE WORK OF THE PHYSICIAN IN THE MISSION FIELD, by *the Lord Bishop of Bloemfontein*	48
THE MINISTRIES OF WOMEN IN THE MISSION FIELD, by *the Lord Bishop of Grahamstown*	51
CLOSING ADDRESS BY THE ARCHBISHOP OF YORK	55

AFTERNOON MEETING

ADDRESS BY HIS GRACE THE PRESIDENT	56
THE CHURCH OF ENGLAND IN THE DOMINION OF CANADA, by *the Archbishop of Rupert's Land*	58
*THE DOMESTIC MISSIONS OF THE CHURCH OF THE UNITED STATES, by *the Lord Bishop of Missouri*	63
*THE FOREIGN MISSIONS OF THE CHURCH OF THE UNITED STATES, by *the Lord Bishop of Kentucky*	66

* Nominated by the Presiding Bishop of the American Church.

in the middle of the day, were all that could be wished. The great Hall was well filled, and interest and attention seemed never to flag. The fifteen papers, following in rapid succession, gave a sort of kaleidoscopic view of the Church and of the Society's work in all parts of the world. When the morning meeting closed with the noble paper of the Bishop of Grahamstown there was no sign of weariness, and when the Bishop of Gibraltar finished his paper, just before five o'clock, the Hall was nearly as full as it had been at any time.

A great number of Bishops were present, and no fewer than seventeen of our Episcopal visitors from the United States attended the meetings. The weighty words of our two English Primates are given verbatim, and it is believed that many persons will be glad to have in permanent form a complete record of the proceedings on this great and important occasion.

H. W. TUCKER,
Secretary.

July 1897.

A SERMON

PREACHED IN ST. PAUL'S CATHEDRAL

On June 23, 1897

THE 196th ANNIVERSARY OF THE SOCIETY

BY THE RIGHT REV.

HUGH MILLER THOMPSON, D.D.

LORD BISHOP OF MISSISSIPPI

"And He said unto them, Go ye into all the world, and preach the Gospel to every creature."—St. Mark xvi. 15.

Yesterday the earth around this great Church shook with the tramp of armèd men, with clang of cymbal, bray of trumpet, and clash of drum ; with banners on all the air, and a roar, like the sea, of the loud leagues of men—a great people rejoicing in its greatness.

And it did well. Since the world began there has been no such Empire. May it stand unshaken till the world shall end—the Imperial Democracy.

There was a parable in the Procession. There was a suggestion only of the power that lies behind, in those forty thousand soldiers from all continents and islands : the fair faces from Scottish heather, English valley, and Irish hillside ; the " dusk faces with white turbans wreathed " from India ; and under nodding plumes the British faces from utmost isles of utmost seas, to symbolise the great dominion. And all in obedience and honour to one gentle, kindly lady who loves not war, nor any strife, whose long life, in her high estate, has been filled only with thoughts of love and peace for all men. I say there was a parable in it : that at last the reign of gentleness has come, that peace is the end of strife, that love is the master, that the war-lords are gone since the mightiest war force on land or sea is held in a woman's hand, and commanded in a woman's name.

And for what is the rejoicing of the land? I have heard the words or read them, and the rejoicing is for wealth multiplied, for power extended, for triumph more and more over the powers of nature, for increase in all material good, for countless hoarded millions, for many laden ships on many seas, for warehouses filled with costly fabrics, for the riches of land and sea!

An official of one colony proclaims the increase of its trade in a few years from one million to thirty, and the cheers shake the roof above his head!

Do I say there is harm in this increase? Surely not, unless one forgets all else in that increase, and then from far off comes the echo of a question which brought ruin to the asker: Is not this great Babylon that *I* have builded?

We are here to bear witness to the abiding truth that wealth and power and vast sovereignty over men do not make a people, that righteousness alone exalteth a nation, that great power means great responsibility, and that the spiritual forces at the last, decide values.

No people ever owed less to their own sense, I think. Almighty God made this people in spite of themselves. He isled His Britain "mid blown seas and storming showers." He hid these islands in the mists and clouds of the roaring North Atlantic. He cut them off from Europe —"the Head of Bran still looking seaward" from the foundations of the White Tower. He warmed them with the soft warm airs and currents of our shores, that drift four thousand miles, and break on these on their way to the Pole.

And in islanding the race He took the responsibility of making the most insular and prejudiced people on the globe! Why, it is only to-day that even the most clearsighted among this people are waking to the fact that Britain is an Empire.

The world has known it for a century, and wondered at the insular blindness. And when a great statesman insisted on giving the Sovereign the only title which could describe her, the proposal was met with a curious amusement. I think she understands it. I think her successor will, and I am very sure neither the people of England, nor the statesmen of England, as far as I can see, in their local politics, have yet come to understand that the Queen of this little realm is an Empress, and Empress of the only true Empire since imperial Rome; that England might be lost—crown, heraldry, and all—in the mighty Empire of Britain; that the little islands might be forgotten amid their seas, and yet the world-shadowing Empire and its imperial crown would still remain.

If one may venture at all to say what Divine Wisdom intends, from a consideration of its acts, then surely God has intended England for His own high and special purposes.

They surely cannot be fulfilled in merely making this people the richest and greatest upon the earth.

For a people's greatness is not in wealth or numbers. It is in the noble, manly men it trains, in the pure and good women who adorn its homes.

Your best men have given this expression in prose and poetry. It is a national conviction.

And then am I rash in saying that the strange story of the race has its divine purpose in this, that England was to be the missionary of the world—the missionary of commerce and the arts of peace, of order and law, of freedom, of guarded homes? But not these only, for without the sure foundation of the religion of the Lord Jesus Christ these cannot stand.

Responsibility is measured by opportunity. Why did Almighty God—my name and yours for "the power behind phenomena"—build this nation of yours?

I cannot see any less, looking philosophically at the world's story, than this clear purpose and intention.

Ringed by the stormy seas; cut off by that happy "silver streak" from war and its alarms; isolated, prejudiced, narrow-minded; you wouldn't mix with other peoples. Your insular prejudice sniffed even at your next-door neighbours, twenty miles away—"God bless the narrow seas that keep her off." God made you the great colonising, empire-building people of the world!

In spite of yourselves you built, by your blunders as well as by your wisdom, another huger Britain with all your laws and literature, and your genuine tongue—a Continental Britain beyond seas.

And you are building more on every island and every continent. You do not hesitate to accept the submission and protectorate, when it is offered, of the realm of some black sovereign—a territory five times the size of your islands.

But what is involved? Only *your* profit—only more wealth for England?

The Christian conquest of every land you take, no less! India? Yes. Who told you to take India? What business had you to take India? But you took it. You assumed the responsibility. England is Christian, so she says. She has given good government to India—a good thing. But England's best thing is her *Christianity*. England's Church to India! That is the only adequate gift.

Your advances everywhere mean order, law, civilization, the rights of man on every sea and shore.

But there are *three crosses* on the flag you float. The flag means Christ and Christ's Gospel. You cannot make it mean less.

The text I have chosen has been used as an argument for conferring *rights*. It does *that* perhaps, but it is more. It is an awful word of the King, the last He left when He took Himself out of His servants' sight for a time, a command to his Church ringing down the ages, resting on every soul, burdening every conscience till He come again!

"We are an Apostolic Church." "Yes," answers the world, "we are glad to hear it, if only you turn in and be an Apostolic Church in truth and fact, a thing the world very badly needs at this present."

I am speaking on the Anniversary of the Society for the Propagation of the Gospel in Foreign Parts, organized under that Command as an expression of the Church's faith and obedience. It is a venerable and noble Society—the oldest Missionary Society in Christendom, the first concrete expression of the Christian conscience on purely missionary duty.

In my land we owe it debts we can never pay. When your politicians and your kings would do nothing, this Society stood by us and helped and sustained.

We owe our early nursing care and protection, which the preface to our Prayer-book mentions, not to the Church nor the State of England. Politicians are an unfortunate set of men, and where they are going when they die (as I hope they all will some day) is as much a puzzle to you as to us. Politicians were in the way—wouldn't give us bishops, because bishops, they thought, must be "lords." Oh, it was pitiful!

And this venerable Society kept working away, and gave us—not your politicians, but this Society—our nursing care and protection, this Society and "good Queen Anne"—good on both sides the Atlantic. In another Queen's reign we cannot forget the glorious reign of the Queen who sent Communion Services to Indian Missions in New York and Canada, and had the Prayer-book and the Gospels translated into Mohawk!

England, with one sad exception, has been so happy in her queens that one might well wish she had the reverse of the Salic law, and allowed only her royal women to rule.

And what are you doing in the work for which England is set? I am told that your revenue from the consumption of tobacco is ten millions a year. Your offerings through all Missionary Societies is somewhat over one-twentieth of your revenue from smoke—*half* a million.

Your luxury increases year by year. I am struck with its rampant aboundingness in the last decade.

I am not speaking of the state and dignity and splendour by which an ancient and famous people rightly adorns its official life. Englishmen always showed the world that, and they did well. Yet of all people they cared the least for personal ease and personal luxury. And now the Spartans are becoming Sybarites! God save the manly heart of England! Prosperity may ruin by seduction a people who, with a banded world against them, were safe under God's hand in the stalwart virtues of a simple manliness.

And with the increase of luxury comes the increase of grinding poverty. Millionaire and pauper are corelative. You are awaking to the terrible reality of a submerged England, and you are doing most commendable and earnest work among your poor. The Church of England is awaking, I am told, to this as never before.

But do you not need special missions to your rich people? When your high-placed people, at this season, flee from the heat and dust, the noise and smoke of London—which is a good thing to do—to their magnificent homes in the country, to spend the Sunday, and kindly take friends with them, do they go, like honest, old-fashioned Englishmen, to the parish church? Do they even, when the home is an ancestral home, and has its chapel, go themselves and take their guests, as did that greatest soldier, the Iron Duke, or that other Premier—
"Good Geoffry, Earl of Derby,
That very perfect knight and gentleman"?

Or do they spend the Lord's Day in the tennis-court, in the billiard-room, in fishing, in shooting, winding up with a luxurious dinner, and the stimulants which too often follow? I am told that this last is becoming common, even among those who, in your union of Church and State, are official as well as hereditary Churchmen and patrons of your parishes.

I think, indeed, that special missions to the rich are needed in my land as well as yours. They are the most neglected class religiously in both countries. They do not even have the Salvation Army to look after them. And we are, on both sides, notwithstanding the parable of Dives and Lazarus, apt to think that wealth, and even respectability, mean moral goodness, and the hard hand and rough jacket mean at least ungodliness—that Lazarus was the man on the road to the flame, not Dives. I suppose some lily-handed priest among us, had he lived then, would have thought special religious care was needed by Him—

"Whose hand was rough, whose hand was hard,
For He wrought in wood in Nazareth town."

Oh, dear friends, all this is not Christian. It is not even English, and surely *not* American.

Are we not both of the race that has won its greatness by the sinewy arm, and the hard hand; that has held "the law of service" the supreme law for heaven and earth; that has reverenced manhood for manhood's sake, because our God is a Man; that has taught us in that old Catechism that to do our duty in that state of life to which " it shall please God to call us," whether it be to rule a nation or to hammer iron into a horseshoe, is equal in God's eyes? And so we rule the nation well, or hammer the horseshoe well; we have done good service under God's high grace, and shall have our reward. Yes, we need special missions to our rich—special missions. They need our help, our sympathy, our pity. They are smothered out of sight sometimes by their riches. They are, many of them, like the poor ass who fell dead under the two panniers of gold (gold is the heaviest of metals); and some of them have been known in sheer despair to kill themselves to get out of their misery. Indeed, in tabulation of things scientifically hereafter, we will have to put down " enormous wealth " as one of the known causes of suicide.

Yet how easily a wise priest or bishop could help the

over-loaded wretch to ease himself of his burden nobly and blessedly!

Yes, I think we need a special missionary effort to save the souls of English and American millionaires—those of them who have yet souls to save!

I am preaching to the clergy—therefore preaching to myself.

Dear brethren, the matter rests with *us*. We must teach the people committed to our charge.

We are timid. Starved missionary treasuries are the fault of the clergy. Let us get rid of cant. We talk stammeringly; we are afraid to appeal. We do our people wrong. They are the noblest, most royal-hearted people on the earth. They want to know their duty and their obligations. It is ours to tell them. They will answer. Don't misunderstand me. I am no pessimist. *I believe* in man, as I believe in God, for my God is a Man. And I especially believe in the men of my own kin. They are a royal people; the masterful, noble people—"the lords of human kind." They rule by right divine on every land and sea. The English cheer—"the short, sharp sabre-cuts of Saxon speech"—are the words of power from pole to pole.

Shall we not do our duty, we clergy, by this glorious people, this chosen people of God? The world is in our hands to-day. The standard of your three crosses, and ours of the azure canton with its argent stars—can bid the world to peace, can bid the world to Christ when we will.

"Clang battle-axe and clash brand;
Let the King reign."

Our wars must be all crusades for "the King," for peace, for goodwill, for order, law, and liberty on all the earth; for the Kingdom of God upon the earth.

And the royal people will always answer royally to royal words. Let us utter them fearlessly. They look to us. Shall *we* fail them? They will give kingly if we ask. These millionaires of ours are so giving. How many millions have been given for Churches, Charities, Colleges, and Universities in the last twenty-five years I am not able to count.

I have none in my poor Diocese; I wish I had. I am quite willing to be responsible for their souls.

Nay, dear brethren, this royal race over whom High God in His wisdom has set us to be shepherds, for whom

He holds us responsible, will never fail us if we trust them. The richest peoples and the greatest—with all their faults, the cleanest, truest, and manliest—have deep down in their hearts faith, reverence, and love for the Man of Nazareth and of Calvary.

They will answer any call in His Name, when those who stand for that Name are bold, honest, and true. Believe in them, they will believe in you. Trust them, they will trust you. I need not say to-day that they are a loyal race, where loyalty can be given. God bless them, wherever over the whole wide world, or all the seas, the men are found "who speak the tongue that Shakespeare spake."

They will always say the manly Christian word. They will always do the manly Christian thing, rude tongue or trained, hard hand or silken, peasant or noble, if they are rightly called and trust the caller. God grant that we clergy be true to them, fair to them, that we manfully put their high place and their high duty plain before them. They owe the world to Christ! no less!

And so this venerable Society can enter on another year of its beneficent work—with all its noble memories fresh and living—with high hope and courage.

It belongs to the ages already. It has stamped its seal on every continent and isle of the great world-empire, and what has grown from that to separate but loving family life. It has expressed the deepest and holiest convictions of the Mother of Nations.

And when many years are gone " in summers yet to be," other faces will be seen and other voices heard in this great Church to testify to its high work for God and men, in other Jubilees of that great people whom, because the Ark of the Covenant abides in her palaces, the Lord hath blessed.

There are two Englands. One, we, your kinsmen from over sea, love with a love and reverence no words of mine can express.

The other we do not much care for. And this other England, I believe, God cares for only as it contains and manifests the first.

For we citizens of your "gigantic daughter of the West" are the first-born of the Lioness of the Isles. We are legitimate children of the line. There is no bar sinister on our escutcheon. And we are proud of it. And we say, "Our little Mother Isle, God bless her," and say, "God save the Queen" with as high hearts as your own.

But it is an ideal Britain that we love: the common mother of us all, the England of Elizabeth, of Bacon, of Spenser, of Shakespeare, of Raleigh: of that gentle, pious pirate, Francis Drake, who first had Morning Prayer said on our shores; of Howard of Effingham; of honest Jack Hawkins, Port-Admiral of Plymouth, who built his ships so well that Drake sailed round the world in one and never started a plank, lost a spar, or split a sail till he dropped anchor under Plymouth Hoe, with the spoils of Spanish treasure-ships, and the ransom of Spanish-American towns—ten million pounds—in his hold, to present to the royal lady whose hand heroes and sages, as their highest earthly honour, knelt to kiss.

That is the England we, your cousins across sea, love with a love burning brighter among us, I think, than among yourselves; the heroic England that had that Empire in her grasp which worthless kings, and more worthless politicians, did not recognize.

There is a grand Divine order in it; that the empire foreshadowed in one woman's reign should wait for another woman's reign to come to reality. That the vision of the heroic age of your isle under the tawny lioness—the solitary soul who would brook no earthly master—should turn to fact in the reign of another woman in happier days and under fairer skies—a happy wife, a happy mother, and a widow with whom all the world has mourned; that the gentle Victoria, with perfect meaning in her name, should see what her imperious, kingly predecessor—the Europe-defying Elizabeth, "the Oath of God" to England and her own high soul—saw only in vision.

And that England is not dead. It never will be dead. With the heroic dust beneath us here we know that the great people have not failed.

You "are not cotton-spinners all." You are not the shop-keepers, pawnbrokers, and money-lenders of the universe. In these capacities the world does not love you. Your own children do not love you. I don't think God loves you.

I stood by his grave in the Abbey the other day—Alfred, Lord Tennyson. One of his Idylls of the King is worth all the cotton mills in England. There are two names cut into the stone in the Crypt Chapel yonder, "the greatest sailor since the world began," and "the great world-victor's victor": Horatio Nelson—Arthur Wellesley.

What is all the wealth of London to these two names, and what do they mean to England and the world?

And no man can go about this royal city and fail to see the nobleness of its princely merchants in long beneficence. The burghers of London have been no vulgar money-grubbers. The royal city has built your Empire royally. A London company gave the world Virginia and New England; London merchants gave you your Indian Empire, and put the Koh-i-noor in the imperial crown of your great Mistress.

Your merchants have been princes. May they always have the princely heart of their fathers!

It is a sight for all the world that here, over your pride of civic wealth, over your banks and warehouses and "the thousand masts of Thames," rises London's own vast Cathedral, and "the dome of the golden cross" casts its shadow over the world's material heart, marks it Christian, claims it for the Lord Christ by the cross above us.

Yes, under your sometimes rough, offensive England, under your sordid, vulgar England, from which your noblest sons have sometimes fled to storm-beaten wilds, lies the high, noble, heroic, *dear* England, to which their hearts turn from your farthest Colonies; to which, after more than a century of separation, our hearts turn with love and kindliness, as to the hearthstone of our fathers.

I am afraid you home-keeping cousins do not know all that this implies. I am afraid England does not know her own greatness, or is scared at the contemplation.

If you were left to your so-called statesmen I should despair, but I believe Almighty God is guiding you, as He has been for many centuries, and that He turns even your follies and ignorances into the uses of His great purposes; that He has had your land, as He has, I believe, my own, under His special care for His own holy ends.

One of our rude American speakers once said, in the hour of our national darkness:—"God needs the United States of America, and He will take care of them." Appeal to the people. They will never fail you. The imperial race wherever found—your side, our side, in Australia, in Rupert's Land—have the kingly heart. It is a tremendous responsibility to be a bishop or priest among the independent, high-hearted, royal race of the world, the men who assert from prince to peasant their own personality, their own individuality, and say: "Here I am before High God, a person before the Three Persons, with my own conscience and my own reason. Your religion and your politics equally must reason with a free man, for I will say my say, wise or foolish, utter my word though the heavens fall."

These people turn Romanists? Then you can have Sirius and the Pleiades and the stars of Orion's Belt purchased by some Electric Light Company to illuminate a railway station or a billiard hall. Afraid? Yes, the imperial people are afraid, but not of Pope, or King, or Emperor. They are and have been for ten centuries afraid only of Almighty God!

MORNING MEETING, JUNE 25

AFTER singing 'God save the Queen,' and prayers, the following ADDRESS OF WELCOME was read by the SECRETARY:

For the fourth time the Society for the Propagation of the Gospel in Foreign Parts is permitted by the authorities of the Church to take its modest share in the work of the august Conference about to assemble at Lambeth, by offering to the Bishops who have come from all parts of the world a respectful and affectionate greeting.

Especially is the Society bound by the memories of the past to offer to the Bishops of the Church of the United States of America the first note of that fuller acclaim of welcome which awaits them from their fellow representatives of the great Anglican Communion whom they will meet in council.

In this auspicious and historic week the minds of all sorts and conditions of men among us are indulging in retrospection, and while others are summing up with due thankfulness and pride the moral and material progress which this country has been permitted to achieve under the good hand of our God during the past threescore years, the present occasion seems to justify, if not to demand, a brief summary of the spiritual progress and expansion which our Church has been allowed to witness, and in which the Society has borne its not inconsiderable share.

In 1837 there were only 7 bishoprics in foreign parts owning allegiance to the See of Canterbury, and in the United States there were 16, all in the Eastern States. The respective numbers now are 92 and 78—170 in all. The way in which our sister Church has multiplied her bishoprics and has followed the Indians and the settlers in the Western States of America has commanded the admiration of the whole Church.

In our own development similar extension can be shown. In older Canada, where in 1837 there were the 2 bishoprics of Nova Scotia and Quebec, there are now 10 dioceses; and westward, where 60 years ago the buffalo and moose roamed at large, and disturbed only by wandering tribes of Indians, over the prairies of the North-West, there are now 7 bishops, of whom some, far removed from contact with the outer world, devote their lives to the conversion of the Indians in their subarctic homes, and others care for the spiritual welfare of the vast immigrant population which have fled from the shores of the Old World to and established themselves on the virgin soil of the New. On the Pacific coast yet 3 other bishops hold the land in trust for the Gospel.

In India, in 1837, 2 bishops bore the spiritual burden of our great dependency, and now 10 bishops serve to bring before the Church the vastness of the field and the need of a large extension of their order. At that time not more than 4 natives of Hindostan appeared on the roll of the clergy, and now nearly 300 minister in sacred things to their own people in the Indian dioceses, and 47 in other lands of the farther East. Where the South African Province now covers the land with its 9 dioceses, 2 or 3 chaplains were the sole representatives of the ministry of our Church in 1837. On the West coast the missionaries of the Church Missionary Society were laying the foundation of the Church at the cost of a death roll unprecedented in any part of the world ; to-day the Native Church possesses its own territory and has 4 bishops, 2 of whom are of African race. On the East coast not a single English missionary was to be found in 1837, and where now the Church Missionary Society and Universities' Mission hold up the banner of the Cross, the whole land was the unchallenged stronghold of darkness and cruel habitations. In 1837 no native of Africa had been ordained; now nearly 150 are to be found in the ranks of the native clergy. In Australia the famous Bishop Broughton, charged with the care of that broad continent where now 14 bishops meet in provincial synod, was ministering to small bodies of settlers gathered in little hamlets which have now grown into mighty cities. In New Zealand Samuel Marsden and his few companions were converting the Maories to the faith ; but four years elapsed before Bishop Selwyn arrived to plant the six dioceses and to originate the glories of the Melanesian Mission.

In the West Indies the two Bishops of Jamaica and Barbados were grappling with the problem of the spiritual elevation of a slave population who had recently obtained from the Christian conscience of England their freedom, and now 8 bishops have succeeded to and have extended their labours.

In this same long period the Colonial Churches, thrown by circumstances on first principles, have provided for themselves systems of synodal action whereby their self-government is assured. A silenced convocation at home gave them no encouragement, but by their own genius and faith in Church principles the happy result which we see has been attained.

Until 1841 the Church of England sent no bishops beyond the limits of the Empire ; now we can point to strong Missions in Borneo, in China, in Japan, in Madagascar, in Corea, and in the isles of the sea.

Woman's work and the healing ministries of the medical evangelist have now become important, almost necessary, factors in the work of Missions, and the labours of the British and Foreign Bible Society, on whose generosity every Mission is dependent, have now given the Word of God in no fewer than 335 languages or dialects.

In all these works the Society has had its full share. The list of fields on which it has entered in the last sixty years is long, perhaps too long, to recite without risk of weariness. In Asia it includes Assam, the Punjab, the Central Provinces, Bombay, Burmah, Ceylon, Cashmere, Borneo, the Straits, China, Japan, and Corea. In South Africa, Natal, the Free State, Kaffraria, the Transvaal, Zululand, Griqualand West, Swaziland, Bechuanaland, Basutoland, Gazaland, Delagoa Bay, Tongaland, Mashonaland, Madagascar, and St. Helena. In America, Rupertsland, Columbia, Honduras, and Panama. In Australasia and the Pacific, Victoria, Western Australia, Queensland, New Zealand, Melanesia, New Guinea, Fiji, and the Hawaiian Islands. At the present moment the Society has the privilege of maintaining 766 missionaries who are teaching the One Faith in 54 languages or dialects in 55 dioceses.

If in this retrospect there be any word of self-glorying, may it be as though it never had been uttered! The thought which it is desired to impress is that there is abundant room for thankfulness for what has been attained, for humiliation at aught that has been done amiss or left undone, and a call, which dare not be disregarded, to go on to higher measures of self-denial and of service.

THE ARCHBISHOP OF YORK delivered the following address:
I believe that I shall best promote the object of this meeting, and also consult both the profit and the pleasure of those who have come together this morning, by limiting within a very narrow compass the address which I have been asked to deliver, for indeed the object of such a meeting as this, and the work for which it is assembled, are best promoted not by theories about Missions, but by records of real Mission work, and such records we shall be privileged to hear this morning from bishops who have come to us from all parts of the world to testify to the great work of God in which they have been permitted to take part. There is one privilege which belongs to me as chairman this morning, of which I gladly avail myself. I mean the opportunity of declaring, not for the first time, not for the hundredth time, my unabated interest in this glorious work of Christian Missions, and also the undiminished confidence in the work which is done by this truly venerable Society. There is one feature in the work of our Society which, although it is perfectly well known to every one of us, is, I think, scarcely kept so prominently in mind as it ought to be. I mean what may be called its dual basis, for there are two great kinds of Missions embraced in the scheme of this Society. There are what I would call Missions of discovery, and there are Missions of recovery. It is, no doubt, the Mission of discovery which attracts the greatest amount of interest. I mean the work which is done in, perhaps, newly discovered or little known lands in seeking to gather in from the deep darkness of heathenism individuals and tribes to the Church of Christ. This is the subject which will, I see, most prominently come before you this morning. But there is another object which this Society from the first has kept steadfastly in view—I mean the need of ministering to our own countrymen who have gone forth from us to make their homes in our distant colonies, and this I am afraid too truly falls under the designation in many cases of Missions of recovery. There are thousands, many of whom may be personally known to those who are present here to-day, who, leaving the salutary influences of help which are within their reach in this Christian country, have gone forth to seek their fortunes, as men say, in distant colonies, and are often very far removed indeed

from any direct influences of religion. The religious spirit within them, nurtured at a mother's knee, gradually becomes enfeebled, and sometimes dies down nearly to extinction. They are often left without any direct contact with a minister of Christ, not only for weeks, but for many months. They are tempted to forget, and I am told that they sometimes do actually forget, the Lord's Day when it comes to them in its weekly course, and thus sinking deeper and deeper into carelessness and forgetfulness, if not into actual lives of sin, they are really subjects for a mission of recovery. I do not mean to imply that in every case, or even in the majority of cases, this is the picture of a colonist's life. But we know very well that the case is not one of infrequent occurrence, and I am thankful—and I am sure that many of you are thankful, and perhaps for personal reasons thankful—that the Society does not forget our own countrymen in these trying and perilous circumstances, but ministers to them according to its power in keeping alive in them the little spark, however feeble it may be, of religious feeling which survives amidst all these perils of colonial life. But it is, as I have said before, the Missions of discovery which no doubt are the most interesting to all of us because there is an element of heroism, of Christian romance, if I may use the expression, connected with them which cannot fail to stir deeply our feelings when the records of such work are brought before us. In looking back over the course of one's own lifetime, over a period of fifty years, at the beginning of which I was living in India and seeing the work of Missions there, looking back on such a period or even on the brief period of nine years which has elapsed since our last Lambeth Conference, I think that we must all feel, and the more we study it the more we shall feel, how great has been the progress in our Mission work. I am not speaking at this moment so much of increase in the matter of results, but rather of progress in what I venture to call the science of Christian Missions. The advance has been greatest in the methods by which the Mission work is done. There was a time (and it is certainly well within my remembrance) when in Missions to the heathen the earliest phase was commonly destructive in its character. The missionary took his stand in the bazaar, denounced the miserable follies of heathenism or the superstitions of Mohamedanism, and tried to clear the ground from all those obstructions and errors before proceeding to the positive part of his work. I believe that we have learned a better way. We have come to recognise more the great principle that there is no branch of the human family in which God has left Himself altogether without witness ; that there is no race or tribe, however degraded, in which there does not still survive some little fragment of Divine truth ; that the Church of Christ, although possessing that truth in its fulness, has no monopoly of it, and that there are fragments of truth scattered here and there even amongst the most savage and degraded nations of the world, and that the discovery of these fragments of truth is the first and the greatest work for a Christian missionary. It is always an easy thing, as we know, to discover evil. It is a far more difficult, but a far nobler thing, to discover good ; and the more the condition of even the most degraded tribes in the world is studied, the more we shall find, and be surprised and delighted to find, these little sparks of truth still surviving beneath the smouldering heap of superstitious fires. Of late a good deal of attention has been given to what are called the sacred books of the East, of India, and of China. There, indeed, it is not a difficult matter to discover the survivals of noble truth, so easily and so much to be admired that some men have been content or desirous almost to place such books as these on a level with our inspired Scriptures; but that is altogether to mistake the meaning of the discovery which they have made. But it is far more difficult in lower forms of senseless idolatry or of sensual worship to discover the truth which lies hidden there. In some of these such vestiges of truth can hardly be detected at all, and men have been so bold as to say that there are none to be found. I absolutely disbelieve this. I believe that wherever the image of God survives in any human being there will be found some little trace of that image in which he is made, and some fragment of the truth which issues from the God Who gave him his being. And I believe that a very great progress has been made in this direction within the last half-century. Men have come to see the beauty and to recognise and to enjoy the happiness of these discoveries of the truth—and I think that there are few greater happinesses in the world—and have built upon them, however minute the fragment may be, the edifice of their Mission work. They have striven to find some common ground, however minute, with those to whom they carry the message of the Gospel—some common ground, however limited in its extent, upon which they can stand side by side with those to whom they are ministering, and from which they may both look upward together to the source of all truth and the source of all good. I believe that principles such as this are more and more influencing the work of Christian Missions throughout the world, and I feel assured that just in proportion as these principles prevail not only will our success in the mere matter of numerical increase be multiplied, but also the roots of the Mission work which we are enabled to do will be more deeply laid, and it is because of my confidence in these principles that I rejoice in what appears to me to be their growth. I feel sure that we shall hear something of it from those who will speak to-day, and I feel sure that I ought not to speak any longer when you have so many waiting to address you whose words you are longing to hear.

THE EXTENSION OF THE EPISCOPATE AND CHURCH ORGANIZATION IN INDIA

BY THE MOST REV. THE LORD BISHOP OF CALCUTTA

IN 1888 I read a paper in this hall on an occasion similar to the present upon the subject of Provincial and Diocesan Organization in India. I am asked to read a paper to-day on the Extension of the Episcopate and Church Organization in India. I presume that this means that I am to carry on the subject of the former paper, to report progress as to what has been done during the past nine years on the lines then indicated, to describe the position at which we have now arrived in the matter of general Church Organization, to express my views concerning the work that still lies before us, and to state what further steps should be taken to make that Organization more complete.

In my former paper already alluded to, I gave a sketch of the history of the Episcopate in India from the year 1814, when the first Bishop of Calcutta found himself the sole representative of the English Episcopate in the whole of the Eastern hemisphere, with India as his headquarters and Australia as an Archdeaconry of his diocese, and brought that history down to the time when the Province consisted (including Colombo) of seven Bishops and two Assistant Bishops. I explained that certain obstacles seemed to bar further development, these obstacles arising from the terms of the Act which in 1833 established the Sees of Madras and Bombay, and made the Bishop of Calcutta to be Metropolitan; but I also expressed my hope that it might prove true, as so often is the case, that though it seems impossible to get over a difficulty, it is found possible to get round it. I am truly thankful to say that that hope has been fully realised—we have got round all the difficulties.

Three bishoprics have been created since 1888, each bishop having his assigned area with full power to exercise his episcopal authority within it, and each one has a permanent independent income provided. Bishop Whitley was consecrated in 1890 for Chhota Nagpur, Bishop Clifford in 1893 for Lucknow, and Bishop Morley in October last year for the whole of the Tinnevelly and Madura district, in the place of the two who were only Assistant Bishops.

The Episcopate, therefore, in the Indian Province now consists of ten Bishops, each one with his territory definitely assigned to him, and each one with his permanent independent income, and I am able to say that we can now go on increasing the Episcopate as seems desirable if only the money can be provided to supply the necessary permanent income. This means that, though in consequence of the varied nature of the conditions under which territory in India is occupied, different processes have to be resorted to, nevertheless, whether it be in British territory or a native state, whether it be in territory acquired before 1833 or since that date, the method of procedure is clear to us, and precedents have been established which have only to be followed in each case as the conditions may require. It is not necessary (even if time permitted) that I should describe in detail the particular points of difference in the processes to be followed, it will be enough to say that seven Bishops of the Province are appointed under Letters Patent, one of these also administering part of my diocese under a Commission from me, two under Commissions from the Bishops in whose diocese the new bishopric is formed, and one under the Jerusalem Act. I have not completed this report of what has been accomplished in India since 1888 in regard to this question of the increase of the Episcopate, until I have made known to you that through the exertions of Bishop Wilkinson 4,000*l.* has been raised towards the endowment of another bishopric which we purpose to locate in the Central Provinces.

Our thanks are due to Bishop Wilkinson for the interest he is taking in the matter, and to this I must add our acknowledgments to the Christian Knowledge Society, to the Society in whose interests we are gathered here to-day, and to the trustees of the Colonial Bishoprics Fund, not forgetting the Churchmen in India and here at home, who have so generously supported the cause of the increase of the Episcopate in India. As the immediate result of the increase in the number of the Bishops, I must next inform you that three new Cathedrals have been built, one at Lahore, another at Allahabad, and a third in Rangoon, and the amount that has been raised for endowment of the bishoprics and the erection of these Cathedrals is, roughly speaking, about 100,000*l.* This is the outcome of that martyrdom of my predecessor, Bishop Milman, when he laid down his life at Rawal Pindi in 1876. I should fail in my duty if I did not further acknowledge the readiness with which the civil authorities both here and in India have sanctioned everything that could be done within the limits of what the law permitted, always provided that no extra expenditure was incurred on the part of the Government: and last, but not least, I must mention with the deepest feeling of affectionate gratitude the support and help of our late Primate Archbishop Benson. I was on my way to Madras with the needful documents signed by him for the consecration of Bishop Morley, when the telegrams brought the news of his translation from earth to Paradise. In God's good providence he was not called away until he had completed this great work for India, in enabling us to solve the at one time apparently hopeless problem as to how to provide for the increase of the Episcopate in that Province.

The provincial organization is rendered effective by the visits of the Metropolitan to each diocese once in five years, and by quinquennial Episcopal Conferences held at Calcutta, when matters affecting the Province are dealt with as the circumstances demand. The organization of each diocese varies according to the circumstances of the diocese; but in all, the affairs of the diocese are carried on by a responsible body elected or selected as representatives of the clergy and laity, and these bodies represent the whole community of Churchmen, European and native together. We have in all these arrangements the germ of that more perfect Synodical organization towards which we are steadily advancing as the Church expands and becomes more thoroughly settled.

The next point upon which I must report is concerning the methods for carrying on our work which during the last ten years have seemed to commend themselves as the result of experience. I need not dwell upon the proved successes of such organizations as the Cambridge Mission at Delhi and the Oxford Brotherhood in Calcutta, but since the creation of the bishopric for Chhota Nagpur, Dublin has sent out a Brotherhood for that diocese; and at Cawnpore there is another Brotherhood, of which two members are brothers of the same family, being sons of the Bishop of Durham. What an example that family sets, for we have four of them in India! The conviction has taken strong hold of us that this associated system is the right one for all our work. The idea has taken firm hold of your minds at home in regard to what is commonly understood as missionary work, the work amongst the non-Christian peoples; but I earnestly desire that it may be recognised that as far as India is concerned it is the sound system for work amongst our scattered Europeans as well—bands of men to be stationed at suitable centres, and thence to work in the surrounding districts, up and down our long lines of railway or in such districts as the tea districts. And when I speak of this as work amongst Europeans I do not mean amongst them exclusively, but work so carried on that the native Christians may be included. I believe that such a combination of work and workers would lead to new opportunities for getting at the non-Christians.

Let us now pass to another branch of our organization which is of the utmost importance—I mean the educational. And here I trust that considerable progress has been made. We have no such difficulties as you have to contend with. Our original basis, under a certain despatch of Sir Charles Wood's in 1854, is denominational, and we are all left to develop our educational institutions on our own lines, receiving assistance from Government both in the matter of building grants and grants towards maintenance under the conditions of an Education Code. I speak at present of education for the children of Europeans and Eurasians. In Calcutta, Bombay, and Madras we have large institutions, one our Calcutta Free School, accommodating some 400 boarders. In the Hills, also, we have large schools, our boys' school at Darjeeling having nearly 200 boys in it. But, as with the providing the ministrations of the Church, so with education; our difficulty is to provide for the children of parents scattered over the districts and stations in the plains—a dozen children in one place, twenty in another, &c. But the greatest difficulty of all is to provide competent teachers, and we are still compelled to draw them largely from home, a very costly system. Here again the crying need is for a teaching Brotherhood, a system under which Churchmen may devote themselves to the work of teaching as men do for Mission work. We watch with great interest the progress of this idea, as it seems to be taking hold of some of you at home. Our Roman brethren have the advantage of us in regard to this department of Church organization, and it is earnestly to be hoped that the English branch of the Church will awake to a sense of the necessity of supplying this want in her system. An attempt is being made with us to establish a general training college for teachers, but I doubt the success of the experiment on undenominational principles. I for my part am most anxious to raise the character of our Boys' High School in Calcutta, and to attach to it a department for the training of our own Church teachers. I should be thankful indeed if some one would offer himself for this special work. Any one with educational zeal and the experience needed for thus building up and crowning our educational organization would find an interesting field for the exercise of his powers, and would be doing a great work for the Church in India.

Concerning the progress of our Church organization in the matter of organizing the native Christian communities, it is a delicate matter to touch upon, the organization under the Missionary Societies being still to so large an extent independent of diocesan organization. In the diocese of Calcutta, the diocesan organization being more distinctly representative, your Society has been able under its rules to hand over to our diocesan council the management of its Missions, and our Board of Missions administers them, I trust, to the satisfaction of your Committee, as assuredly we think it does to the increased efficiency of the work. I am quite confident that the native Christians themselves appreciate their more definite connection with the diocese. In the other dioceses progress is being made towards the same arrangement so far as your Society is concerned. As regards the Christian communities who are indebted to the other great Missionary Society for support, they are organized on the Society's own lines, and will, I suppose, remain outside the diocesan organization until they become independent of pecuniary support from home and can act for themselves. I have no desire to say an unkind word or to leave an impression that I think lightly of the splendid work the Societies are doing, but if I am to speak of the organization of the Church in India, common honesty compels me to report how seriously this variety of system stands in the way of unity on the basis of diocesan organization, and many of the intelligent native Christians are conscious of it. That in one city, say Calcutta, the native Christians in the north of it should be organized on one system and those on the southern side of the city upon another, must cause confusion, to say the least of it, and does give cause for anxiety as to the future. Bishop Morley has a most interesting and difficult work to do in bringing the Christian community in Tinnevelly into one body under one organization, and I trust that he will be heartily supported by both Societies.

For the present we must all work steadily on, carrying out conscientiously our own convictions as to the course to be followed. God has brought us safely through many difficulties, and He will show us the way through this one if we are faithful. May He also stir the hearts of the Church at large to the removing of the greatest difficulty of all—that of finding men to work the machine as it is so far organized, and the means of maintaining and developing that organization on true Church lines.

MISSIONS TO THE ABORIGINES OF INDIA

BY THE LORD BISHOP OF CHHOTA NAGPUR

INDIA is often called Hindusthán, or the place of the Hindus. It is, however, well known to most of you that the Hindus came into the country some three thousand years ago, and found other tribes living there. These tribes we call the Aborigines, although they also were immigrants in earlier times. The aboriginal tribes were driven before the more powerful Hindus into the wilder and more hilly parts of the country, and are still found in the neighbourhood of the Himalaya and Vindhya Mountains, and in the hills of Southern India.

These aboriginal tribes are very numerous, but I need not attempt to give the names of all or even of many of them. It will be sufficient to mention those among whom the more important Missions are located. These are: (1) the Hill Arrians, in the Diocese of Travancore; (2) the Gonds, in the Central Provinces; (3) the Santals, Mundas, and Hos, these three being nearly related; and (4) the Uraons and Paháris. These are in the Dioceses of Calcutta and Chhota Nagpur. Besides these I may mention the Khasias in the hills of Assam, among whom a very good work is carried on by a society of Welsh Nonconformists.

I will ask you to bear in mind that what I say has special reference to the Aborigines of Chhota Nagpur, but holds good in the case of other such tribes who have similar characteristics, customs, and religious ideas.

The religion of these people may be called Demonolatry, having for its object the propitiation of malignant spirits, who are supposed to be very numerous and bloodthirsty. The Demons, or Bhúts, have at times a great craving, and worry people by causing pain, sickness, insanity, or death till they are satiated with the blood of some animal. Fowls, goats, or pigs are slaughtered; the blood satisfies the Bhút, and the flesh supplies a feast for those who offer the sacrifice. Generally speaking, anyone can perform the sacrifice, but in some cases this has to be done by a village official. A knife, axe, or sword is commonly made use of, but small fowls and pigs are sometimes held by the legs and killed by having their heads dashed violently on the horns of the cattle for whose preservation they are offered. It is frequently necessary to call in the aid of a professional, a kind of Bhút detective, in order to ascertain which particular demon is causing trouble, because all are not to be treated in the same way. Some demand the blood of goats, some of pigs, others have a taste for that of fowls of a special colour.

The Bhúts are sometimes stirred up by evil-disposed people, whom we may call witches, to injure others, and there are professional witch-finders who are consulted by those who have reason to think themselves the objects of enmity. This system of course affords great scope for false accusations, and those who are pointed out as witches are often ill treated and forced to fly from their homes. Formerly many of such unfortunate people were murdered. The Bhúts, however, do not always wait to be set in motion by witches, but act of their own will, and thus get many innocent people into trouble, who are driven to seek refuge in the Christian Church. Some of these malignant beings are supposed to be attached to special places or families or individuals. We may call these private Bhúts, and they occasion great annoyance to their hosts. A man or woman may be free from all suspicion of evil intention, and yet, if their demon be named by the detective as the cause of trouble, they have to square him by a sacrifice which often involves the outlay of more money than they care to spend.

The spirits of the dead sometimes become Bhúts, and cause great alarm ; but of the state of those who have departed this life the survivors have very indefinite notions, and these supply no sanctions which have any influence on their lives. It is sometimes stated that the Aborigines of India do not recognise distinctions of caste. This statement is too general. Some of them certainly will not eat or drink or intermarry with persons of another tribe, or of some subdivision of their own tribe. This may be the result of contact with Hindus, whose claim to superiority and purity seems to have a great attraction for their less civilised neighbours. It is not uncommon for men of these tribes to attach themselves to some professional spiritual guide, to give up eating beef, put on the sacred thread, and adopt the worship of some Hindu divinity. The Hindu system admits of almost unlimited compromise, and Aborigines have been largely absorbed into the lower castes. There is great reason to fear that many of these tribes, if not drawn into the Christian Church, will become Hinduised.

In some important characteristics the Aborigines compare favourably with other inhabitants of India—*e.g.* more or less in truthfulness and honesty, to a much greater degree in cheerfulness. They take a great delight in dancing with a drum accompaniment, and in many villages there is a special place set apart for this amusement, which at some festivals is kept up not only all night, but till the sun is high next morning. Among the Uraons of Chhota Nagpur a house is built close to the dancing place, and in this the young unmarried men of the village sleep. The songs sung at the dances are often, though certainly not always, indecent. Drunkenness is almost universal on some occasions, but it would be a misrepresentation of facts to describe the people as habitual drunkards. It will be regarded as a natural consequence of such conditions that sexual immorality among those of the same tribe is very common and easily condoned.

All these Aborigines were quite illiterate, not even having a written language. They possess, I think, an average intellectual capacity, and arrive at a fairly high standard when their education is commenced when they are young.

The mass of the people are very poor, but their wants are so few that there is but little real distress, except in times like the present, when the crops have more or less failed. Many of them suffer a good deal of annoyance and oppression from the more acute Hindus or Mussalmans who own or lease their villages, and who are not deterred by any scruples of conscience from using the somewhat expensive legal procedure which our Courts provide, for the ruin of the unsophisticated cultivators of the soil. This oppression, together with the claim on the part of the landlords to a large amount of unpaid labour from their tenants, has given rise to a long-continued agitation in Chhota Nagpur. These agitators have a very simple creed. 'Our ancestors,' they say, 'cut down the forest, and brought the land under cultivation long before these aliens came among us ; therefore all alien landlords and leaseholders ought to be turned out, and we will pay them no rent.'

All that I have said so far is closely connected with my subject, ' Missions to the Aborigines of India,' for it will enable us to understand on the one hand some of the hindrances to the spread of the Gospel, and on the other hand some of those conditions which have tended to favour it.

Among the hindrances to Mission work we may place first of all the total absence of all sense of spiritual needs and aspirations. When a heathen in my Diocese is asked concerning his religion, he says plainly that he is 'of the world,' and not a Christian. He lives wholly for this world, and by his sacrifices seeks only relief from temporal ills. Then the love of drinking intoxicating liquor, and the frequenting of the dancing places in the villages or at fairs prejudice the heathen very strongly against Christianity, for Christians are expected to abstain from these things. We constantly advocate total abstinence from intoxicants, although we cannot make it a condition for baptism. The divisions of Christendom, made manifest by the missionaries of different denominations working in the same district, are often stated to be a hindrance, but I do not think the aboriginal tribes find in these any serious stumblingblock, though they certainly involve a great waste of power and money.

The fear of the malignity of the Bhúts acts in two directions ; sometimes it deters men from embracing a religion which forbids sacrificing to demons, but often it leads men to seek for protection from their malice by adopting Christianity.

Among the conditions favourable to the propagation of the Gospel among the Aborigines of India we may place the great want felt by them of some sure protector. The revelation of an omnipotent and all-loving Father, who is ever ready and able to take into His Kingdom all who will come, meets a deeply felt want. Many persons in our Lord's time on earth felt only the need of temporal relief, but were led on to seek salvation from sin. It is still so. The frequent demands for sacrifices to propitiate the demons often make men weary of the whole system of heathenism. Then there is the entire absence of a definite system of religion claiming authority. Men rightly feel that they should not lightly give up the beliefs and customs of their ancestors, but beyond this sentiment the people we are concerned with have nothing to bind them to their old faith.

The oppression of the landlords may certainly be named as tending to make men favourably disposed to Christianity, which hates oppression and robbery, and teaches the Fatherhood of God and the brotherhood of men, especially of those who are of the household of faith.

Then again there is generally that absence of prejudice against Christianity which, in the case of Hindus and Mussalmans, often leads to the persecution of converts. My experience goes to show that the Aborigines who become Christians usually gain in social position; instead of being despised they are looked up to, and by availing themselves of the opportunities for education they become the more intelligent and independent members of the village community. A neater and cleaner dress and a brighter and more intelligent expression of countenance is often sufficient to enable a stranger to distinguish a Christian from a heathen.

Among the causes which dispose men to seek admission into the Christian Church may be mentioned sickness or other affliction, which is ascribed to the malignity of Bhúts by the heathen, but from which deliverance is sought from God by Christians. The expense involved in sacrifices, accusations of witchcraft, and complaints of mischief caused by Bhúts connected with persons who are not suspected of malice, also induce people to sever their connection with heathenism. Those also who suffer oppression, or who are involved in quarrels or law suits, not unfrequently seek a closer connection with a European missionary, or with the Christian clergy or teachers, whose independent position enables them to stand up against oppression, and who may assist their less intelligent brethren by their advice or influence. Others are led to seek admission into the Christian Church because it seems more reasonable to worship the beneficent Creator and Preserver of mankind, than to rest content with the often obviously futile endeavour to propitiate evil spirits by sacrifices. Some such motives predispose men to seek for instruction in the Faith; they come with minds prepared to believe what may be taught, and find eventually more than they either sought or desired.

It would be clearly impossible to condense within the limits prescribed for this paper any history of missionary work among these aboriginal tribes, although the oldest Missions were established only about fifty years ago, and others much more recently. I must use the few minutes which remain for some account of the organization of the Church among these people. This, of course, is in various stages of development.

All those who are engaged in the work are, I believe, quite agreed that schools are of the first importance. Without these teachers cannot be provided, and an indigenous ministry cannot be raised up; and without this the work must lack permanence and efficiency. Small village schools form a foundation; the central boarding schools carry on the education of a selected number to a higher standard, so that students are enabled to make some use of English books; and recently the Dublin University Mission has opened a High School in which Christian education is carried up to the standard of the Calcutta University Entrance Examination. This is as far as we have got at present.

A considerable number of schoolmasters, teachers, and clergy have been trained in the C.M.S. Missions among the Santals, and in the

S.P.G. Missions and those of the German Evangelical Lutherans in Chhota Nagpur. A very pleasant and, I trust, profitable intercourse has been initiated between the brethren of my Diocese and those who are connected with the C.M.S. in the country of the Santals and Gonds. At the request of the Bishop of Calcutta I have visited the Missions in Santalia for Confirmation and Ordination, and on two occasions Santal candidates for Holy Orders have been sent to Ranchi. Some leading men from the Gonds and Santals have also visited us, and have, I believe, carried away very pleasant memories of a hearty reception by their brethren of Chhota Nagpur. Some teachers sent by us to work among the Gonds have been a valuable help to the C.M.S. clergy who are labouring in the Central Provinces.

Eleven priests and five deacons, all natives of the country, are working in my own Diocese, none of whom are dependent on the funds of S.P.G for their stipends. The schoolmasters and teachers who are under the supervision of these clergy do depend on our venerable Society, and must do so for some years to come. One native priest has been sent to Assam to minister to the very numerous Christian emigrants from Chhota Nagpur who work on the tea plantations. The teachers keep diaries of work, and go to the pastor of their district once a week for report and to receive instruction. Once a year they go into Ranchi, our central station, for some weeks' instruction by the European missionaries. Forms containing abstracts of the diaries are sent in monthly by the teachers, and quarterly reports are sent to the Bishop by the clergy.

Cases seeming to require the exercise of Church discipline, and these are not infrequent, are in the first place investigated by the clergy in consultation with the leading members of the congregation; if they are found to involve exclusion from Holy Communion, the Bishop's sanction is required. This also is required before readmission to Christian fellowship. Cases of this kind are most frequently connected with sins of impurity, or with complicity in sacrificing under fear of the malignant demons. The indissolubility of Christian marriage, which is of course strictly maintained by us, involves conditions which are sometimes felt to be very hard to submit to by those who, in their heathen state, had very lax notions on the subject.

I do not know the exact number of the Aborigines of India who profess Christianity; it is probably about 100,000, and the increase seems to vary with the number of missionaries who are sent out from Europe to propagate the Gospel among them.

I am quite conscious of the very abrupt and fragmentary style of my short paper. Many points have been left untouched on which information may have been desired and expected, and much of what has been said is of limited application. For this I claim your indulgence, as my experience, though somewhat long, has been confined within a narrow sphere.

I will only add an earnest request that you will sometimes commend to God's special grace your brethren in Christ among the aboriginal tribes of India, and will pray that He will guide and bless those whom He has sent to minister to them.

THE CHURCH IN JAPAN

BY THE LORD BISHOP OF SOUTH TOKYO

(*Read by the Rev. S. Bickersteth, Vicar of Lewisham,
in consequence of the illness of the Bishop*)

ANGLICAN Missions in Japan have this special interest attaching to them, that they are carried on in a country which is as independent politically as the lands from which they are sent. More than half of the continent of Asia has, during the last hundred years, been brought under the control of European Governments. Scarcely a year passes (the current year is not an exception) but sees some extension of this process; nor does it seem likely that the principles which are at work to produce this end will at any time cease to operate. But the island empire of Japan with its 45,000,000 of inhabitants is outside their range. The independence of character of its people, their insular position and considerable resources forbid the thought that Japan will ever be among the lands where the influence of Europe or America will be politically dominant. Moreover, since the recent successful war Japan has become conscious of her position and power in a way which was not the case before; and this position has been in fact recognized by the new treaties which come into force two years hence.

On the other hand, Japan alone among Eastern nations has voluntarily opened her heart and life to the influence of Western ideas, and in the incredibly short space of thirty years succeeded in assimilating no small part of that external civilization which with us is the result of centuries of labour and struggle.

In a country like this it would be natural to anticipate rapid movements and counter movements of opinion. And such are continually taking place. Let me refer to two recent instances.

i. At the time of the last Lambeth Conference, nine years ago, an indiscriminate enthusiasm for all things Western held possession of the public mind. Not only European art and science, but Western dress and Western customs generally were widely adopted, and voices even were raised in favour of a national profession of Christianity as the religion of civilisation. This movement was succeeded by a strong and, in many ways, I believe, a healthy reaction. The violence of the reform had offended the deep sentiment of Japanese patriotism, and it was rightly felt that while mechanical inventions, such as railways and telegraphs, can be transferred from land to land, it is otherwise with customs and beliefs. These, if they are to be of value, are the expression of an inner life, the formularisation of individual convictions. They cannot be transplanted wholesale from continent to continent or imposed from without by legislative enactment. This reaction has not yet spent its force, and it may be doubted whether, in the long run, Christianity will be found to have lost anything by it.

ii. Closely connected with this movement in favour of 'things Japanese' has been a revival during the same period of interest in the ancient religions of Japan—Shintoism and Buddhism—and a fairly sustained effort on behalf of the Buddhist priesthood to retain what survives of their ancient influence. New temples have been erected, one in the ancient capital city of Kyoto costing, it is said, a million sterling. Buddhistic schools have been opened and magazines published. 'Drawing-room meetings' in the interest of Buddhism are, I am told, not unknown. This revival has probably affected very little the cultured classes of the country. It is and will remain powerless against the great system of Government education. But so far as it implies any renewal of interest in religious questions among the masses of the people, by the Christian missionary it is rather to be welcomed than deprecated. Bigotry and error in religious belief are less formidable than lethargy and indifference.

On the other hand, if time permitted, much might have been said of the advance of unbelief among the educated Japanese, whether in the direction of agnosticism or of unitarian negation.

But the bare mention of important movements of thought and opinion of this kind may be sufficient to suggest a not incorrect view of the conditions under which the work of the Church is being prosecuted in Japan.

Plainly under such conditions, humanly speaking, no immediate results can be expected on a large scale among the upper classes. I ventured nine years ago in this hall to describe the attitude of the educated Japanese in reference to Christianity as one of 'respectful hesitation.' I fear that as a class they are no nearer to its acceptance now than they were then. Many of the present leaders of Japanese thought were passing through their schooldays when a generation since came the great Revolution which placed Japan again in contact with other lands. The education which in those old days they received was based on the Confucian classics, that is to say, they were taught a high system of morality apart from any form of theological belief. The natural result was that their religious aspirations and instincts were wholly uncultivated. The younger men have been trained under the modern system of education, but from the religious point of view the exchange is in no way for the better. The universities and high schools of modern Japan know nothing of religion under any form or in any guise. Can it be a matter of surprise that a leading Japanese politician, now representing his country at a European court, wrote the other day: 'The age in which we live is a scientific age, and such questions as the existence of God, Hell, Heaven, and the soul excite no more real interest than the discussion of such abstract topics as time and space. I am a believer in the existence of a fine type of morality without any religion, and as long as instruction in practical morality is an essential part of the educational system of the country we have nothing to fear.' It need not be said that so long as opinions like these are rife the trend of thought will be opposed to those feelings and instincts which make for ready acceptance of the Christian Faith. Better things must be looked for not suddenly but through the conversion of one and another to a better mind by the grace of God, and through the influence which such converts will gradually exercise upon their compeers.

Meanwhile, now, as of old, the Church will find a far less encumbered field in the lower and middle classes of society. Among them the ancient religions of the country, specially Buddhism, have always maintained, in whatever sadly misdirected forms, a certain standard of religious feeling, and this may be expected, as the number of Christians and Christian teachers increases, to seek its true satisfaction and end in the revelation of Christ.

In this connection it is a matter of thankfulness to be able to record that while at the last Lambeth Conference the number of Christians connected with the Missions of the Anglican Communion in Japan was about 1,500, it is now over 6,000. This indeed is a very small number of believers as compared with the millions among whom they live, and they are scattered over the whole Empire, living alone or in little companies, from the semi-arctic region of the Hokkaido to the tropical islands of Loo Choo and Formosa. Very various were the means by which they were won. Some by school teaching or reading Christian books, some by listening to public addresses, some through words heard and acts of kindness received in Christian dispensaries—the majority probably by personal intercourse with those who were Christians before them, whether foreign missionary or fellow-countryman, that intercourse for which Japanese life offers so many opportunities, when the little group gathers round the brazier in the evening to discuss the events of the day. For the most part these Christians are poor and without social standing, but they are all (with the exception of those who are directly employed in Mission work) independent of the foreign Missions as regards their means of support, living the ordinary life of Japanese craftsmen and artificers, clerks or school teachers, among their own countrymen, exposed in consequence, need it be said, in the atmosphere and surroundings of heathenism, to innumerable temptations, but possessing unrivalled opportunities of winning their brethren to Christ if their conduct is at one with their faith. As regards opposition and persecution a distinction must be drawn between their legal position and their actual circumstances. Legally by the new constitution of the Empire they have the same rights of protection and toleration as the Buddhists or Shintoists. Actually nothing can prevent their being often the victims of harsh treatment and much social annoyance, the hard but salutary portion of early converts.

These Christians, by whatever Mission—American, Canadian, or English—they have been evangelized, all form one duly organized Church with its own constitution and canons. Each congregation has its vestry and sends its representatives once a year to the council of the missionary diocese. Each diocese, of which now there are six, has its own council and societies for missionary and pastoral work, which are recognized and assisted by the foreign Missionary Societies; and once in three years the canons require that there should be held (in Tokyo or Osaka) a general Synod of the whole Japanese Church. The meetings of these Synods, whether diocesan or general, are often occasions of no little interest. Perhaps the most important subject which hitherto has come before the general Synod has been the acceptance of a Book of Common Prayer, which combines, we hope, some of the good points of the Books in use both in America and England. The Japanese clergy now number about thirty, and at the Synods have the right to vote separately from the laity—a right which also attaches to the Bishops—a very necessary provision in assemblies which in time to come may discuss important matters of discipline or doctrine.

The number of foreign missionaries (clergy and ladies) in connection with the Anglican Communion is about 90—a most inadequate number for carrying the Gospel to 45,000,000 of people.

Moreover, one result of the recent war has been to lay upon the conscience of the bishops and clergy in Japan a great additional responsibility—the evangelization of the island of Formosa. On this there is no time to dwell. The last meeting of the Lambeth Conference saw the establishment of the Diocese of Corea. May it not be hoped that from the present gathering one outcome may be the establishment of a missionary diocese in Formosa? The first trained workers for such a diocese must be drawn from the Church in the main islands of Japan, and must always be united with it in closest bonds of sympathy.

It is then on these few thousand scattered converts in Japan, on this Church, organized but not yet financially independent or socially influential or numerically strong, that our hopes for the future are fixed. In it we ask your interest and prayers, and for it we plead for far more adequate support in time to come.

THE MISSION TO COREA

BY THE RIGHT REV. BISHOP CORFE

I. ON the creation of the diocese in 1889 the S.P.G., by means of a liberal grant of 1,500*l*. per annum, made it possible for the Bishop to ask for volunteers to accompany him to a field of labour which had never before been occupied by missionaries of the English Church.

The Bishop, having relinquished his income as a chaplain on the active list of the R.N., felt that he could invite others to follow his example and to come and share with him the grant which the Society had placed at his disposal. The invitation was accepted by those who followed the Bishop immediately to Corea, and by all the agents of the Society who have come to Corea since, who have found that a sum of between 75*l*. and 80*l*. per annum, including an allowance to each of 1*l*. a month for clothing and pocket-money, suffices to maintain them in health and comfort. The result of this has been that a great deal of the Society's grant has been available annually for the building of churches, and for the purchase or adaptation of houses to serve as homes for the missionaries or for schools or for orphanages as the need for them arose. Accordingly through the instrumentality of the Society there have been bought or built in Corea, since 1890, two churches, one church room, two parsonages, one school, and six mission-houses—which last stand in compounds sufficiently commodious to admit of the houses within them being used as hospitals, dispensaries, schools, orphanages and a printing office.

With regard to the Manchurian Province of Shing King, which, since its addition to the diocese in 1891, has formed with Corea one jurisdiction, the Society has aided it by an annual grant of 150*l.*, and a permission to spend 400*l.* of the Special Fund which it administers for Corea upon the purchase of a property in the treaty port of Niu Chwang large enough for the erection of a parsonage house and church. The one missionary who has been working there single-handed for four years, having after great difficulty at last found suitable ground, is now engaged in building this house, and hopes that there will be a small sum over to form the nucleus of a church. So much for the method which, with the consent of the Society and the willing co-operation of its agents in the diocese, has been adopted by the Bishop in regard to the yearly expenditure of the income derived from the Society.

II. The Bishop left England nine months after his consecration and reached Corea on the feast of St. Michael's and All Angels in 1890, leaving his clergy to follow him as soon as they could be released from their engagements in England. There are four ports in Corea which have been opened by treaty and in which, therefore, it was evident that the work had to be begun. Each of the four was visited by the Bishop, with a view to seeing what were the claims it afforded for the commencement of the work. And here the Bishop had to be guided by two considerations. His clergy and candidates for the ministry were, like himself, wholly ignorant of Corean, and required a period of two years' uninterrupted study before they could safely undertake any serious evangelistic or literary responsibility. This was the first consideration which had to be faced. And the second was the fact that the Society's work is addressed first to English folk and then to the heathen. When, therefore, it was found that in only two of these treaty ports there were any members of the Church of England, the Bishop determined to centralise his forces in them, and from the outset to provide regular means of grace for such as would receive them ; whilst, by the aid of native teachers, the missionaries were studying the language. And, in order to free them as much as possible from interruption in their studies, he placed them all in a large house in the heart of the capital, putting the English work in charge of a priest who had unexpectedly joined the Mission from Canada, and who, being past middle age, did not expect to make much progress with Chinese. In the Port of Chemulpo—which is only 24 miles distant from Sycoul, the capital—the Bishop himself took charge of the English service. In these two ports, then, at first in temporary and then in permanent buildings, the Sacraments have been administered and the Word of God has been preached regularly within two months of the arrival of the Mission in Corea up to the present time.

III. But in addition to the necessity of learning Chinese and Corean there was the need of providing a Christian literature—some parts at least of the Bible and Prayer-book, without which it was evident that no evangelistic work—for which a Bishop was to be responsible—could be begun. They who had to use the Word of God and the Book of Common Prayer in their ministrations must address themselves to the task of providing for their needs in this direction as soon as their own studies in the literary language of the country enabled them to do so. That work is even now hardly begun, and its success or failure in the future as in the past will depend not on the number of the missionaries engaged on it, but on the skill and aptitude and above all the patience which they bring to it. Owing to losses from one cause or another, the Bishop has now only two members of the Mission staff who are competent translators— the Rev. M. N. Trollope, his chaplain, who came to Corea in the spring of 1891, and an American doctor who landed in Chemulpo with the Bishop six months before. These two missionaries combine a very accurate knowledge of the vernacular with a large and continually increasing acquaintance with classical Chinese ; and on their shoulders rests the future of biblical and liturgical translations for the Church of England in Corea. Before leaving Corea I placed in Mr. Trollope's hands a translation of the greater part of the Prayer-book and more than half the Psalms, on which I have long been engaged. It is to be feared, however, that this MS. will not save our translators trouble—will, indeed, serve but little purpose beyond showing how I have been occupied and emphasising my conviction that in translating the Word of God and the prayers and praises of the Church we, both clergy and laity, of this generation shall find our principal task—the task which whilst it demands most patience from ourselves will be most remunerative to our successors. Since leaving Corea I have had the privilege of making the acquaintance in Shanghai of Bishop Schereshewski, of the American Church, whose liturgical translations have long been a classic amongst missionaries in China, and who, now crippled by paralysis and long since retired from active ministry, has caused himself to be carried from America to China in order to complete and see through the press his new translation of the Holy Scriptures. The sight of this venerable man, so helpless in limb and speech, so vigorous in mind and faith, engaged in this task was a most wholesome object-lesson to us impetuous young missionaries.

IV. But the question will be asked—Is the Society to see no other results during this generation than a series of translations ? Has nothing come to the Coreans themselves of this close contact with them for seven years ? It would seem as if the missionaries of even this generation were to be allowed to see the beginnings of the spiritual building whose foundations they are laying. It is very early to speak of such things, and I desire to speak of them with becoming modesty. Last June, I was informed that seven or eight adults, nearly all of the poorest class, or of those who were dependent on the Mission, had shown signs of something more than self interest in the inquiries they had long been making of the Society's agents into Christianity. Accordingly I prepared an office for the admission of catechumens, and on Christmas Eve I admitted them to the catechumenate. These were followed a few days after by three or four women. On the same Christmas Eve I baptised five little orphan boys who had long been under the charge of our doctor at Chemulpo. For these catechumens a catechism has been prepared and printed. On the morning of that Christmas festival the first instalment of the Prayer-book in Corean made its appearance, when, at Syeoul, in the Chapel of the Resurrection (which had been waiting six years for it) Coreans heard for the first time, in their own tongue, the Church Litany and Office of the Holy Communion to the end of the Gospel. Most of these catechumens live on an island close to the mainland, between Syeoul and Chemulpo, which has been occupied by one of the Society's agents for some years. To meet the developments—if any—in this quarter, a church room has been added to the mission-house capable of accommodating thirty or forty worshippers. Thus, there are two chapels built by the Society, in which, when I left, the Church's services were being regularly held for Coreans. And to these two centres, St. Michael's, Chemulpo, must be added as a third. Chemulpo has no resident missionary in Holy Orders; but for the benefit of the little orphans in his charge the doctor has been made a lay reader, and collects his little flock daily in the church.

V. A night school for the study of English, opened in 1890, at Chemulpo, by the doctor, at the request of certain Japanese and Chinese residents, gave place after the war to more direct mission work amongst the Japanese by a layman who came to relieve the doctor of labours which, in addition to his medical work, proved too arduous. Last autumn we were permitted to see the first fruits of this, when (after a valued visit from one of Bishop Bickersteth's clergy) five of these Japanese inquirers were admitted by the Bishop as catechumens, and shortly after were baptised and confirmed. But this work struggles on with great difficulty, owing to the absence of a clergyman to superintend the lay reader, and to undertake the responsibility of this important work amongst the Japanese in Corea. At present, the Bishop and his clergy have to perform their ministrations by means of the Japanese Prayer-book, of which they understand not one word. A priest to undertake this Japanese work, and, at the same time, to minister to the English congregation of St. Michael's, is now the great pressing need of the Corean portion of the diocese.

VI. As to Manchuria there is very little to report. Of Mission work amongst the Chinese none. Through the kindness of H.B.M. consul, a room has been allowed us in which, for five years, the Church's services have been held without the intermission, I believe, of a single Sunday. The present chaplain is a devoted man, and his devotion is appreciated by the residents. But beyond a short annual visit the Bishop has hitherto been unable either to relieve his solitude or to satisfy his missionary aspirations. So eager is he to see at least the beginning of missionary work amongst the Chinese of the province, that he has asked my permission to build in the Mission compound, at his own expense, a small hospital for women, for whom gratuitous medical treatment has been promised by the local practitioner, if I can get the 70*l.* a year which will be necessary for its maintenance.

VII. In conclusion, the friends of the Society must bear in mind that Corea and Manchuria are two separate countries, between which there can be no interchange of missionaries; that in Corea the Society has, at present, eight agents—in Manchuria one; and that to enable me to discharge my duties to Manchuria, I have come to England to seek help from the Archbishop of Canterbury. Whether the Society will be permitted to do for Manchuria what it has done for Corea, it is not for me to say. But enough has, I hope, been said to show that, whether in Corea or Manchuria, I am deeply indebted to the Society, whose operations in every part of the world I commend to your prayers and work.

THE PROVINCE OF SOUTH AFRICA

BY THE MOST REV. THE LORD BISHOP OF CAPE TOWN, METROPOLITAN OF SOUTH AFRICA

THE subject allotted to me is a sufficiently comprehensive one. It covers a space of over a million square miles; and, if it only embraces a period of just fifty years, yet they are years of no small importance in the history of the Colonial Church. The title of my subject is 'The Province of South Africa.'

This is the year of anniversaries. The whole British Empire is rejoicing in this the sixtieth year of her most gracious Majesty's reign; the whole Anglican Communion is commemorating the 1300th anniversary of the arrival of St. Augustine, to which may be added that of the beautiful death of St. Columba; and the Church in South Africa is keeping, in a modest and simple fashion, its own Jubilee, in which it is vain enough to think it deserves the sympathy and congratulations of the Church from which she sprang, and of which she is not an undutiful nor, we hope, an unworthy daughter.

The fact that this is our Jubilee, and that within four days the actual fiftieth anniversary will dawn upon us, as on the dioceses of Melbourne, Adelaide, and Newcastle, naturally invites me to cast this paper into the form of a retrospect of the last fifty years. But I am warned off by remembering that, if I were to do so, I should be repeating to a very considerable extent what I read from this place nine years ago, and should also be telling you a story with which you are already for the most part familiar.

I will therefore merely say that the original Diocese of Cape Town has now grown into ten; that the 13 clergy which Bishop Gray found have increased to more than 300; that for the last twenty-seven years provincial and diocesan synodical organization has been in full operation and is continually growing in importance and in general estimation; that by a carefully adjusted system of checks, requiring the joint assent of bishops, clergy, and laity, precipitate legislation is rendered impossible; and that, while we claim for the Church the right to interpret her own standards and formularies, independently of the civil power, yet we have pledged ourselves to retain those standards and formularies intact, and to do our utmost to promote the establishment of a central tribunal, in order that, as far as possible, unity may be maintained in matters of faith and doctrine throughout our widespread communion. These pledges are the best answer to those cavillers who have never ceased to denounce the Church of our province for encouraging a spirit of independence and separation in respect of our Mother Church.

When I last read a paper from this place I expressed an earnest hope that two new Dioceses would soon be formed which should link our work on to, and bring us into immediate touch with, our brethren of the Universities' Mission. This hope has already been fulfilled. The translation of the late Bishop Knight Bruce to the diocese of Mashonaland, and of Bishop Smythe to that of Lebombo, has completed our province, so far as one can at present judge, and has, nominally at least, covered the ground right up to the Zambesi River, where we join hands with the Diocese of Central Africa. This is something to be thankful for. It is the fulfilment of a hope which did not appear then at all likely to be realised so soon. For the endowment of Lebombo we are very largely indebted to the indefatigable efforts of Bishop T. E. Wilkinson, formerly of Zululand, now the Coadjutor to the Bishop of London for North and Central Europe. It is gratifying to be able to state that at least one half of the endowment of Mashonaland was raised in South Africa. In both cases we have been very largely assisted by the Colonial Bishoprics Fund, by the Society for Promoting Christian Knowledge, and not least by the Society whose festival we are keeping to-day. But the creation of missionary sees is of little value if their bishops are left unsupported by clergy, and the dearth of clergy in both these Dioceses is quite saddening, considering the enormous area and vast heathen population of both of them. England, too, must not forget how of late years she has been pouring her own sons and daughters into Rhodesia by thousands. I can only describe it as a perfectly appalling and heartrending fact, that Bishop Gaul and his friends in England have been for many months urgently entreating men to go into his Diocese, but that no response is made. The voice cries, but it is apparently to a bare wilderness. There is not a sound to break the silence. Will no one offer himself to-day?

While speaking of missionary work, I cannot leave unmentioned the loss which our Church has incurred since the last Lambeth Conference in the deaths of three of our most devoted and able missionary bishops— Henry Callaway, a man of wide experience and high intellectual gifts; Douglas McKenzie, the firm friend of the Zulu race and the lover of their children; and George Wyndham Knight-Bruce, the ideal pioneer of the Church's work; these have all passed to their rest, two of them having been previously forced to abandon active missionary work through ill health, and the Church mourns their departure, even while it still relies upon their intercessions, now more effectual even than before.

Looking back over the past few years, since the last meeting of this kind, there is one thing which ought to be recorded with thankfulness. It is the growth which has been made in the spirit of union amongst ourselves. I always felt that the ecclesiastical dissension of fifteen years ago was far less serious than it seemed. There was singularly little in it of any breach in the law of Christian charity. If we differed, the difference scarcely at all affected our private friendship, while mutual explanations and the healing process of time have done a great deal to remove the barriers which had arisen, and to ease the strain and tension between us. The agitation of that time has now practically ceased, and we have, I think, settled down to carry on our Church's work in the spirit of unity and concord, and on the lines laid down in our Provincial Constitution. Even in Natal there appears every reason to believe that time has done much in this direction, and that the conciliatory, yet decided, policy of the Bishop of Natal during these last years (alas! that grievous sickness prevents his being with us to-day) is slowly accomplishing the work of amalgamation. It is devoutly to be hoped that the Conference at Lambeth will take a particular step which may have the effect of making that union complete. It will not be the fault of the South African bishops if it fails to do so. Another cause for thankfulness is the growth amongst the laity, poor and rich alike—a growth which I believe is going on throughout the province—of a sense of responsibility for the material support of the Church's work. In Cape Town I have especial opportunities for noticing this growth, and the improved organization throughout the parishes of the Diocese is very largely encouraging it. But I have good reason for believing that in every Diocese the same spirit is manifesting itself. No doubt it is a process which requires time for its full development, but it *is* going on; and the ideas which those who have lived under the shadow of an established and largely endowed Church bring out to the Colonies with them, that the ministrations of their Church ought to be supplied to them without cost to themselves, whatever their circumstances may be, are steadily disappearing. At the same time, we are bound to remind those who remain at home that they retain for their own benefit all the endowments and church buildings which our common ancestors have provided; that we of the English Church in South Africa are in, I suppose, almost every Diocese only a small proportion of the European population, and that the members of our Church in some of the Dioceses are outnumbered, by four or five to one, by the members of another Communion, to whom nearly the whole country belongs, and who were in possession of it a century and a half before it became a part of the English Empire. In a word, our Church is the Church of a very small minority. It is, I know, often felt and said that, with all the wealth that South Africa produces, the Church there ought to be independent of all external support. I reply that, if much wealth comes out of South African soil, it does not remain for the most part in South Africa. It mostly comes to Europe, to fill the pockets of shareholders in this country or in others : it is seen in stately buildings in the west of London, or in delightful country residences; it swells your Church collections, and is given in large amounts to your hospitals and other philanthropic objects. But little of it remains in the country whence it is extracted, and what does remain is very largely in the hands of those who have no interest in the welfare of our Church. The wealth is yours, not ours, and forms an additional ground for your helping the Church in the land whence many of you derive your incomes.

A word or two as regards the future. The great need now is, not to create fresh Dioceses, at least for the present, but to strengthen the work in those which exist. Even in the older and more settled Dioceses this need is great. It may surprise you to be told, but it is true, that, according to the last census, there are still as many heathen and Mahomedans in the Cape Colony as there are Christians. I suppose in Natal and in the Transvaal the proportion of heathen is greater still. In all these Dioceses, moreover, and especially in the larger ones, such as Cape Town and the Transvaal, there are numbers of people of English birth, living in remote places, who cannot be reached by the ordinary parochial ministry. Itinerant clergy must be provided—but funds are required. Along the line of the goldfields in Johannesburg the need of clergy and devoted lay workers among the miners is most urgent. No grander field can be imagined for missionary work. There are hundreds and thousands who would welcome it, and are perishing from want of it. We need there hardworking, soul-loving men who will devote themselves to their own spiritual work, who will accept the political position as being, however painful, yet the sphere in which God, through the course of outward circumstances, has called upon them to labour, and who will not waste their energies or mar their influence by engaging in political agitation. The laity are not backward in providing an income : it is the men who are wanting.

Let me, in conclusion, ask your sympathy and support in erecting in Cape Town, as the metropolitical city of the Province, a beautiful, stately cathedral, in place of the undignified and unsightly structure which Bishop Gray on his arrival found already built (though it was only in part paid for, the balance being taken up in shares), and which he was compelled to accept for his cathedral as the only considerable church in the city. For fifty years has this most unimposing building remained the cathedral church of the capital of the Colony and of the metropolis of the Province. There is an unanimous feeling both within and without the Diocese that the time has come to wipe away this reproach, and to erect a church which shall adequately represent to our own people and to strangers the beauty of holiness, and the idea of the dignity of Christian worship. In a land which has no ancient history and no architectural landmarks, and which has few churches that are not almost mean and commonplace, we feel more and more the need of having something in our churches to inspire men with the feelings of awe and reverence, and, above all, of a church of this kind in the chief city of the Province, and in the midst of a population of about 80,000 souls. I can imagine no more fitting monument than this of the fifty years life of our Church, and of the fiftieth anniversary, four days hence, of the consecration to the office and work of a Bishop in the Church of God of Robert Gray, first Bishop and Metropolitan of the Church in South Africa, who laid the foundation fifty years ago of a spiritual temple which may, in God's good providence, become in ages hence the spiritual home of all the manifold races in the Southern regions of the 'dark continent.'

THE WORK OF THE CHURCH AMONGST THE NATIVE TRIBES OF SOUTH AFRICA

BY THE LORD BISHOP OF ST. JOHN'S

Beginnings.—We began to evangelize them during the first decade after the founding of the Sees of Capetown, Grahamstown and Natal, in the Dioceses of Grahamstown, St. John's (then a part of Grahamstown), Natal, and Zululand (there are no natives, properly so called, of the Bantu race in the Diocese of Capetown); and in the following decade amongst the people of Basutuland and Bechuanaland, all situate in the Diocese of Bloemfontein, though widely separated in distance and characteristics. In each case the commencement of Mission work followed closely on the founding of the episcopate. The work, therefore, may be said to be forty years old among the Xosa, commonly called Kaffir, and Zulu; and thirty years among the other great division, the Basutu and Bechuana.

Characteristics.—The Kaffirs (Xosa) and the Zulus are nearly related; their language is very similar, their habits and customs almost identical. Those of the Zulus have been modified during the present century by their military organization. They all show the same strong spirit of conservatism and persistence of purpose; and though they have been most isolated, most of the tribes composing this section of the race show a willingness to travel and enter the service of the white man.

The Fingoes are a link between the Zulu and the Kaffir. Zulu in origin, they have learned the Kaffir dialect and customs. Of them I shall speak directly.

The Basutus are more industrious, more naturally disposed to agriculture and the arts of peace; are generally unwilling to leave their country; their body politic has a very strong controlling power; they are very loyal to their chiefs. As a nation they are peace-loving, though excellent fighting men; they are more receptive of new ideas than the other sections of the race: they assimilate much of our civilization more easily.

Obstacles.—The difficulties which stood in the way of the spread of our teaching were:—

1. The power of the chiefs, who felt by a sort of instinct, and doubtless

a right one, that every convert was a soldier lost to them, a real loss in the old days of incessant intertribal warfare.

2. The disturbed state of the country caused the early missionaries to begin the system of 'Mission stations'—*i.e.* considerable tracts of land reserved for the use of the Mission; a system which had its use, but one which always has the effect of making the influence of Christianity conterminous with the boundaries of the Mission station.

3. Polygamy. The hostility of a system so at variance with Christianity is obvious; to it is probably to be attributed the large excess in the number of women who have embraced Christianity.

Effect of annexation by British.—During the last twenty-five years, one by one, all the native districts have passed under British rule. This, while an advantage in some cases, means a distinct loss in others. Much of their old environment, which gave a vigour to their character as a nation, has passed away.

Loss.—(1) The 'pax Britannica' has robbed them of the self-reliance of the men who had to defend their families and cattle with their strong right hand.

(2) The freer food-supply, the result of peace and European implements of agriculture, does away with self-denial and self-restraint in the matter of food. The young children were always taken care of when food was scarce. Now it seldom is scarce.

(3) The substitution of our laws and methods of procedure for theirs has taken away from them the interest which was so keen in their lawsuits, which were pleaded in the crude courts of their chiefs. Now the litigants are commonly represented by law agents, who do not spare them in the matter of fees. They learn to lie in giving evidence. They did not dare before, for they would be inevitably entrapped in the keen cross-questioning. And bribery is becoming common, which was impossible when cattle were the only wealth.

Gains.—They are freed from the deadly blighting influence of the 'witch doctor,' under whom no one dared to differ from his neighbour; any prominence, a better house, or too many cattle, would bring down the accusation of witchcraft.

Education is encouraged by Government; conditions of life are easier; public works give good wages; there is protection to life and property; intertribal intercourse is made possible.

The power of the chiefs has been broken down, and so obstacles have been removed to the conversion of individuals; a man can follow his natural bent.

Methods.—Mission Stations.—The plan on which the earlier missionary went, was to ask for a grant of land from the chief, on which he built his house and church and school; and such natives as desired to be instructed would gather round him, and live under such regulations as might be put in force. Heathen practices were forbidden; every one must go to church; the children must go to school.

This plan filled the schools and the church; but the type of Christianity was wanting in stability very often, though *some* excellent

Christians were made in this way. The great disadvantage seems to be that the influence of the Mission was confined to the boundaries of the Mission land ; it did not spread.

This was the way in which Missions were begun in Grahamstown, St. John's, Natal, and Zululand Dioceses. Among the Basutus and Bechuana a more healthy method held from the beginning. No doubt the intense conservatism of the Kaffirs and Zulus made the Mission station system almost a necessity. It seemed once almost an impossibility for a man to lead a Christian life outside a Mission station. He would have had no friends, he would have been a pariah, a fair mark for the accusation of being a sorcerer and worker in the black art. At the same time, I believe it would have been wiser to have worked on on faith until the tide turned, and have been content with infinitely small results.

The Mission station formed a sanctuary for the unfortunate people who were 'smelt out;' their lives were saved, but they were not often desirable sort of people to have on the station. Often the residents on the station were all ranked under the name of 'sorcerer' from this fact. The chiefs always respected the sanctuary of the Mission.

System of scattered Christians.—Amongst the southern Kaffir tribes the healthier system began at St. Matthew's, Keiskamma, and in the Mission district of St. Mark's ; in the latter case, outside the bounds of the large Mission lands given by Kreli.

Among Fingoes.—In both cases the new plan began among Fingoes, among whom the tribal bond is much laxer. They are Zulu by origin, and came south driven by the great conqueror Chaka in the beginning of this century. They took refuge among the various tribes through whom they passed—Pondos, Tembus, and Xosas—who treated them, some harshly, some kindly.

In 1830-35 the great mass of the Fingoes, as they were called (a name equivalent, apparently, to 'refugee') passed westwards, across the Kei into the colony, where most of them took service amongst the farmers. When the Kaffir war broke out, they did good service against the Kaffirs, whom they had always looked upon as their enemies, and were rewarded by being given tracts of country. Notably, in 1865, a very large number were placed across the Kei, eastward, in the land forfeited by the Galekas, a country called now Fingoland, some fifty miles by thirty. But as these territories have been gradually annexed, they have passed on northward, wherever they could find land to settle in amongst the tribes : for they will never pass beyond British protection. It is amongst these people that the healthier type of Mission work, among the Kaffir speaking tribes, began. There was none of that intense tribal feeling. The English had saved them, and made them rich, and they would take, as far as could be, our ways, our thoughts. They willingly sent their children to school ; they came to church ; converts were made ; and wherever they went, as they spread over the valleys and hills of the country which was allotted to them, they took their Christianity with them.

Growth of Native Ministry ; it arose with the need.—Among these little Christian communities a sturdier sort of Christianity arose ; they felt the responsibility of their position ; they had to keep up the standard of life amongst themselves. Leaders were appointed, men of character, influence and piety, who held service on Sunday, and reported all matters to the European priest, on his monthly round.

Out of this state of things, these scattered Christian communities, arose the need of a native ministry ; and from these men, who were found thus to fill the gap, as lay workers, has been found chiefly the material to supply that need. Some of the number of this important band have been specially trained from their youth ; but probably most have been selected, called, as far as the human call goes, for their moral power, their fidelity, and the efficiency of their work as lay workers, working for the most part in more or less isolated positions ; but in every case special instruction has been given, either at college, or under a theological tutor or his parish priest ; and I think but one spent some time in England at St. Augustine's College.

This ordained ministry numbers at present between thirty and forty members, which is, roughly speaking about 1 in 1,000 native Christians. I am unable to give the exact numbers ; but my estimate of our native Christians is between 30,000 and 40,000. This excludes the considerable number of coloured Christians who live in the Diocese of Capetown and elsewhere, who do not belong to the Bantu race, and are therefore outside my present subject. This ordained ministry is what I should call the upper stratum of a very much larger number of lay workers, catechists, schoolmasters, many of whom, indeed probably most, act as readers and preachers to the heathen ; a number amounting probably to more than three hundred.

It is worthy of note, that among the natives of the two southern Dioceses of Grahamstown and St. John's the ministry has principally been supplied by the Fingo race, to which I have just alluded ; and it would seem that this race has been placed amongst us, under God's providence, for this very work, to be the missionary race of Africa. They are high-class people, being Zulu race by origin ; they are freed from the bonds of tribal influence ; they are great colonisers, restless and pushing, their enemies call them grasping ; and lastly, it must be noted, they are the result of English influence. They were made what they are by contact with us, and are therefore tougher and hardier for the contact ; more seasoned, if I may say so, than the raw tribes who have not yet been exposed to the deadly influence of our civilisation.

Quality of our Native Christians.—And what of the quality of our native Church ? What results have accrued ? How are they influencing the destinies of the race ?

It is difficult to estimate the internal results ; but one thing we can speak of, that a Christian conscience has grown up. We who have had to deal, with a close spiritual touch, with our people, know that this is so ; that the difference is enormous between raw heathen idea of sin and that displayed, during a quiet talk, with one of our Christians. In the one case the faculty is asleep, but we know well the signs of true sorrow for sin in the latter ; their spiritual sense is very really alive. As heathen they have but little or no idea of reverence ; but many have borne witness to the reverence of a Christian congregation.

Purity.—Has their Christianity an influence on conduct? Certainly it has. Lax as is often their morality, in the restricted sense of the word, they have the Christian standard before them, and we know the strivings of many to keep up to it. The heathen have no standard and no strivings.

Theft.—The old national proclivity to steal the farmer's stock, a survival, it is to be remembered, among the heathen, of the old war feeling, is with Christians almost unknown. A well-known resident magistrate told me that among the 5,000 native Christians of the district he had never had one convicted of theft. And Christian natives have been used, in a well-known instance, to put down stock-stealing, by being placed in a belt of country between European farmers and a heathen tribe : the experiment has been a success. Further, witness has been borne by many to their loyalty ; notably a man in high position asserted in my hearing, in the most emphatic manner, that the Christian Fingoes saved Fingoland from rebellion in 1880. He was chief magistrate of the district.

Humility—that delicate flower of the Christian character—we shall be told, has not yet blossomed on this soil. No doubt there is, and must be, a tendency to pride, when the half-educated native compares himself with his heathen father. But they are in a transition state ; they have not yet learnt to tread securely in their new surroundings ; their eyes have not yet learnt to judge of the proportion of things. Certainly our best men and women, those most deeply influenced, shine distinctly with this grace.

Temporal progress.—The Christians are the people of progress ; they are the most advanced in agriculture, and trade flourishes where they are ; for their wants are many and varied compared with those of the heathen.

Prospects.—The outlook is sufficiently encouraging in the older territories, and in the new. Our want in the future will be well-trained native clergy and lay workers, to carry the gifts to the heathen now coming under British influence.

They are crystallising under new forms, and we must take advantage of the crisis. The iron, God's rough material, is glowing for the forging ; the blast, the fury of the nations, has been raising it to a white heat ; even *now* it will be on the anvil. Are the hammermen ready ?

THE WORK OF THE PHYSICIAN IN THE MISSION FIELD

BY THE LORD BISHOP OF BLOEMFONTEIN

MINISTRATIONS to the sick bodies of men formed a prominent feature in our Lord's work on earth. And when He sent His Apostles forth to preach the Gospel of the Kingdom, He gave them also 'authority to heal all manner of diseases.'[1] Nor was this confined to the time of our Lord's earthly ministry. It was included in the commission given to the Apostles after the Resurrection,[2] and among the Ministries of the Holy Spirit in the Church we find St. Paul mentioning gifts of healing.[3] It would perhaps be not unfair to regard the command 'heal the sick' as coming under the general authority and charge to preach the Gospel to every creature—to make disciples of all the nations.

The Gospel was to touch not the souls only, but also the bodies of men. The Christ was to bring light and life to the whole being of man, to be the Saviour not only of the soul but also of the body. This may be regarded as the Gospel of the Incarnation: for the Eternal Son, taking on Him the whole nature of man, showed that it was His purpose to raise it wholly, and not in part only, to the perfection for which it had been created by Almighty God, and 'to as many as received Him, to them gave He power to become children of God.'

For the inauguration of the new kingdom special powers were given to the Apostles and to others in the first ages: powers relating to the mind and soul, including the gift of divers languages; and also powers relating to the body, including that of healing the sick. But by degrees these extraordinary powers were withdrawn, and the Christian teacher had to rely on his ordinary faculties, enlightened, directed and energized by the Holy Spirit working through the common channels of human knowledge and skill. Even so, it still often occurred that the same individual was called and endowed for the care of both body and soul—the best physicians were often to be found among the ecclesiastics, and this continued till comparatively modern times. The founder and first President of the Royal College of Physicians of London was a priest.[4]

It might at first sight be supposed that the best way of carrying on the missionary work of the Church would be to continue or to revive this double character of priest-physician, so that the same missionary might, as did the Apostles, tend and heal both soul and body. But this has been gradually increasing in difficulty in the present age, and now it has become practically well-nigh impossible. There has been, on the one hand, a vast increase in the store of human knowledge in regard to disease and its treatment, together with a very wonderful development on the techni-

---

[1] St. Matt. x. 1.   [2] St. Mark xvi. 18.   [3] 1 Cor. xii. 9.
[4] Sir Thomas Linacre. It appears, however, that he did not take Holy Orders until late in life.

cal side of medical and surgical science, requiring special skill and training for its application. And, on the other hand, there is a growing appreciation of the intricacy of the problems involved in Mission work, so that it is recognized that the preacher of the Gospel to the heathen needs special study and preparation beyond that required by the ordinary Christian minister.

Any one who does his duty in a sphere of reasonable size, as a physician or surgeon, finds the demands on his time and energy well-nigh, if not quite, all absorbing, and it is next to impossible for him to be at the same time an efficient Mission priest. I know there are those who combine both works efficiently, but they are, I think, notable exceptions to the rule.

In places where society is organized on a Christian basis, the provinces of the priest and the physician respectively are more or less clearly defined, and they may, and often do, work harmoniously together, the latter recognising the nobility of his calling and the greatness of his responsibility as carrying on part of the work of his Master Christ, and carrying it on with the same end in view for which Christ Himself undertook it. The same is true to a certain extent in countries or districts, like Basutoland, where medical officers are appointed by the Government in each magistracy to minister to natives as well as to Europeans. True missionary work may be carried on by all these medical men within the bounds of their own calling, if they rise to their opportunities and devote their knowledge and skill to the promotion of the highest welfare of the people among whom they work, at the same time preaching to them by the example of consistent Christian life. To this end religious influences brought to bear on students of medicine by societies like the Guild of St. Luke are of the highest importance.

But in places beyond the pale of Christian civilization, where our missionaries go to preach the Gospel to the heathen, these missionaries are not able to carry out the commission of their Master in its fulness unless there are some among them who have received the 'gifts of healing.' It is true that some good may be, and is, done by ordinary missionaries in Holy Orders having some knowledge of anatomy and physiology and of the laws of health, some training how to act in accidents and emergencies, and how to use simple remedies, where no skilled medical aid is at hand.

But far more than this is needed. If the spirit of our Lord's command is to be obeyed, we must have as high a standard of medical knowledge and skill in the Mission field as we desiderate of fitness for their work on the part of the missionary clergy. In a properly organized Mission we need—and here I am about to quote the words of a distinguished London physician, Sir Dyce Duckworth—'the co-operation of *fully qualified* medical men who would, under episcopal discipline, do what was set them to do. Half-trained (so-called) medical missionaries,' he goes on to say, 'are of no use, and a complete training costs a good deal.' To these emphatic words I would add that such men must be *true missionaries*. They must not go out for two or three years with a view of getting some special experience and then returning to practise in England. They must be men (and women) called to give their lives to the advancement of the kingdom of our Lord and Master. There is no reason at all why such devotion should be supposed to be exclusively associated with the vocation to the Sacred Ministry in the case of men or with that to life in a sisterhood in the case of women. Thank God, the possibility and the actual existence of such devotion is being recognized now in the Church of England ; but it does seem to need something more in the way of organization, or some means for stirring up devotion, and of turning it into right channels, and of using it to the best advantage when it is aroused.

The S.P.C.K. has done and is doing very good service in supplying funds for the training of medical men and women for this great work ; but altogether the number of medical missionaries connected with our great Church societies is very small in proportion to the need. Statistics in 'Medical Missions' for January 1896, of medical missionaries holding British degrees or diplomas, gave the number connected with the Church Missionary Society as 30 ; S.P.G., 8 ; Church of England Zenana Society, 3 ; Universities Mission, 2 ; while the different Presbyterian bodies in Scotland and England together had 71, the London Missionary Society 20, and so on. The numbers have doubtless in some cases increased since then, especially in the case of the Zenana Society, and now it is to be noted with thankfulness that the Women's Association connected with the S.P.G. is taking up vigorously the subject of medical Missions to women.

It seems to me desirable that medical men who are engaged as missionaries should be admitted by the Bishop to the office of Reader in the Church, so that they may, under proper sanction, conduct services, and help in other ways in directly spiritual work.

And I would venture also to suggest that as in England it is not considered inconsistent with the calling to the Sacred Ministry that some men should give most of their time and energy to school teaching, so it would not be unreasonable for a medical missionary in special cases to be ordained to the diaconate, or even to the priesthood, still giving most of his time to his medical work. In such cases he would ordinarily, while supreme, of course, in his own medical department, be subordinate to the priest in charge of the Mission, as regards the exercise of his ministry to souls.

In conclusion, I desire to say, I undertook this Paper not from any conviction of my fitness for the task, but because it was laid on me by those to whose judgement I felt bound to defer. And as I am unable to speak with the authority of experience on medical missionary work, I have endeavoured rather to suggest the principles on which I conceive such work ought to be carried on. And I trust that nothing I have advanced will be found inconsistent with the fundamental laws of the Missions of the Catholic Church, which are based on the great commission given by our Lord to His Apostles.

THE MINISTRIES OF WOMEN IN THE MISSION FIELD

BY THE LORD BISHOP OF GRAHAMSTOWN

IN the onward movement of this age, so largely influenced by the life and rule of the Royal woman upon her Imperial throne, few can fail to note the growth, in idea and application, of woman's mission and work in the Kingdom of our Lord.

Twenty-two years ago I read a Paper in a Conference promoted by this Society, somewhat in the tone of apology and vindication for the right and necessity of woman to be duly represented in the Mission field of the Church. Now it is everywhere recognized, that a Mission cannot be fully organized, even in its early days, without women on its staff of workers.

I. On our S.P.G. stations, as well as in connection with other Church Societies, in India and China, Japan and Corea, in Africa, East and South, lives and souls of the women of various peoples and languages are now being touched and moulded by Christian women. On the Church of England Zenana Mission, I am informed, there are 200 English and 310 Native women workers, and the contributions in aid of that Mission, including legacies and special funds, amounted in one year to a total of over 33,500*l*. The income of the Women's Mission Association in connection with the S.P.G. last year came up to a total of only 6,893*l*. 11*s*. 6*d*. for the support of 74 English and 85 Native teachers. This is not as it should be. Let the income be doubled in thanksgiving and reparation, so that appeals from all the world around may meet with a worthier response.

II. The ministries and relations under which we find women on active service in the Mission field, speaking generally, may be grouped in four divisions, as—

i. Wives of missionaries.

ii. Detached and individual workers in more or less direct relation to missionary clergy or societies.

iii. Deaconesses.

iv. In religious communities, whether of branch houses in connection with English Sisterhoods, or in communities of local growth.

The number of missionaries' wives must in the nature of things be limited; but in all these other spheres of work the demand for workers is at least a hundredfold in excess of the supply. It would take thousands of Christian women workers to lift the Hindu women alone out of degradation.

i. I should be the last to belittle by comparison with other vocations that of the wife and mother in a missionary home. In pluck and patience she is not seldom among the first of heroines. If only she has a real sympathy with the people and the work, she may be a great power for good. There is no better civilizing and purifying influence than that of the really Christian home of the Mission priest, whether among natives or colonists; but then it must be really Christian in tone, with the fire of the missionary spirit glowing at its hearth. It is true that she may have to realise, more even than her husband, what it means to take up the Cross daily, in loneliness and isolation from her fellows, in straitened circumstances, and often, perhaps, in lack of the means for the proper education of her children; but she may have the reward of being a minister of light and love, and the trusted friend of many sisters whose lives without hers would be dark and hopeless. It is remarkable that, in spite of all the trials in the missionary life, it is chiefly the sons of missionaries amongst our colonists who have come forward for the ministry of the Church.

ii. Excellent work has been done in time past, and is being done, as I can myself testify, by ladies not attached to any order or special office. They may come as members of a body of teachers or nurses, making their own arrangements with the Mission authorities, and in most cases very rightly requiring an adequate salary. Without the aid of such helpers, in schools or hospitals, the Church would be greatly the poorer in every part of the world. In whatever capacity they are engaged for Church work, for our sake and their own happiness, they should come out, not as merely nominal churchwomen, but understanding the reason for their being members of the Church. Religion must rest on principle, and be more than a decoration and sentiment. There is comparatively little to sustain character or conviction in the conditions of a new country. It is difficult to realise, until we are away from them and thrown upon ourselves, how much we depend upon our surroundings, how little we often may have of our own in the way of foundation. A great drawback with this class of workers is that continuity is imperiled, and often, there is not sufficient opportunity for previously testing capacity and endurance.

iii. Of Deaconesses it is rather too soon, so far as the Mission field is concerned, to say much. There is unquestionably a need for such special service as they offer, and it is surely meet and right that women should be drawn to a ministry so venerable in origin and so capable of adaptation. It is a sphere in which those who desire to dedicate themselves unreservedly to the service of the Church, and who are yet not attracted or suited to life in a community, may realise their vocation. They go forth with the benediction and commission of the chief pastor, and promise, on their part, obedience to ecclesiastical order in duly subordinate and appropriate ministrations. The Bishop would naturally require a guarantee of satisfactory training, and proof of modest, humble, and diligent preparation. Two deaconesses are at work in my Diocese; one lately come; of the other, who has been long with us, the praise is in all the district where she is working under the parish priest.

iv. On the ministry of Sisters, and of ladies associated with them, in relation to colonial and native Missions, I feel I can speak with some authority, as, in the providence of God, I have been intimately connected with that branch of work for more than a quarter of a century. In order to illustrate the capacity of a Sisterhood as a missionary agency, I will instance one, which I know thoroughly, as an example.

The Community of the Resurrection, in my Diocese, was founded in 1884, and has now grown into a society of 27 Sisters, with whom are associated 38 workers. Nursing and parochial visiting, industrial work, and the care and training of neglected children, who are thus guarded from evil that might involve rescue work in the future, are duties for which they are responsible; but their chief work is that of teaching, and there are now two Normal schools, one for training native teachers, under their guidance, and about 1,000 children of all colours and classes being taught by them.

The late Bishop French, of Lahore, writes (Life, vol. i. p. 201): ' I see more and more that schools form the very stamina of our Mission efforts, and that the daily instilled lessons leave an impression which, though long and determinedly resisted, is never wholly lost. May this lead me to fervent daily intercession for them.'

It is essential that the quality of work for the Church, whether moral or technical—and all the more if it be a free-will offering to God—should be thorough, and of the very best, better even than if it were paid for at the highest current rates. But it is not after all by the amount of work in hand, nor by its cheapness that the blessing brought to a Mission by a community of Sisters is to be measured. It is in the witness for the royal claims of Christ upon life, and for the homage due to Him; it is in the power brought to bear by continual intercession upon all missionary agencies around; it is in the 'embracement of eternal life,' and of the heavenly reward evidently set forth; it is in epistles to be known and read of all men of the 'doctrine of the Cross reduced to life;' it is in the rest and gladness of soul that has found a home for ever in the Church of the Living God; it is in the patience of the Kingdom, which is exhibited in the continuity of order where work is not wholly dependent on the enthusiasm of the individual.

In the Colonies and Mission field, where every venture for the Kingdom of God stands out in unshaded light, it is even more important than in England to provide proper safeguards against the infirmities incident to all Church agencies, and those peculiar to this special ministry. Just because the corruption of the best is the worst, it is most needful to have such bulwarks as the Church's wisdom may devise. I can only indicate a few of these now.

1. There is need for hearty recognition of the life as a vocation on the part of the Church as well as formal recognition of a particular Order or House on the part of the Bishop whose office it is to be visitor.

2. Before the rule or constitution is formally adopted, the sanction of the visitor should be required, and care taken that the rule of the superior be made constitutional.

3. The tenure of office by the superior should be for a term of years —say five or seven only—and the election periodical.

4. The right of visitation should be practically exercised by the visitor, and an appeal be open to him from the Sisters.

Though it is necessary that the rule for the Mission Sisterhood should not be too rigid, it should be well observed. Its chief aim should be to promote simplicity with straightforwardness in devotion as well as character, and a community spirit with a view of forming a true family life in a home in which those who have given up earthly homes of their own should find sympathy and affection. There is a certain tendency in Sisters under some rules to become hard.

5. It is very important that there should be lay co-operation, especially of treasurers and auditors in regard to all funds raised by subscriptions or given for definite purposes.

6. The assent of the parish priest and of the Bishop of the diocese should be required before a branch is started in a parish or diocese.

The reserve, however, of a Sisters' home should be not less respected than that of an ordinary Christian family or household. As a matter of experience I have found that the idea of consecration and devotion to a Living Risen Lord and Master, rather than to the image of the dead Christ reproduced, has a mighty influence in creating the true spirit of self-sacrifice, simplicity and perseverance.

As a testimony to the felt need of such a ministry, I may quote a word of strong appeal from a letter of Bishop Gaul of Mashonaland, who writes : 'Do pray urge on them at home the crying call there is for *Communities* in the Colonies—make them realise what it is in a new land like this to have strong bodies of Roman orders pervading the educational, nursing and even social life of the country, whilst the Church is represented by three nurses for the whole of Rhodesia.'

Oh ! for an imperial enthusiasm in the hearts of our daughters, and for a passion for their Church !

A further advantage which a community of Sisters possesses is in supplying a centre and home and protection for ladies, who are willing to be associated with them in fellowship and in good works, without being in any way directly or indirectly pledged to become Sisters or to permanent separation from their homes. The aid that such workers may give is invaluable, and even visitors for a short time, bearing their own expenses, can help greatly in keeping up interest and sympathy. But if any would be indeed a fellow-helper with the Gospel of the Kingdom, let her give herself first to the Lord in singleness of heart. It is not that we ask for a strained or sanctimonious religiousness. Where religious zeal is rooted in personal devotion to the Living Christ and in loyal allegiance, for the truth's sake, to our mother Church, the qualities of an active mind, an even temper, good spirits and a sense of humour are all to the good. Let her be restful too in the essentials of ritual and of spiritual privilege, if no more can be had, and not forget that it is very easy to pull down, but most difficult to build up ; that to be critical, in the day of small things, of feeble beginnings, is more smart than true and generous ; and that to do the best with what is imperfect, and make the best of what is on the way to nobler achievement, is the part of the faithful and royal hearted.

In the magnificent commemoration of this week you have delighted to do honour in banquet and procession to the state officials of various nations and peoples who own our Queen as Sovereign. 'Each for all, and all for each' has been the fact behind the pageant. After this week,

I trust, you will never speak of sons and daughters, who go out for Christ to our Colonies, as going away to 'foreign' parts ; it is only to another territory of your Imperial Home—and Empire means service, and wider Empire larger service for Christ and commonwealth. And even if your dear ones go outside our Queen's dominions in the name of the King of Kings, it will only be to extend the bounds of Jerusalem, which is the mother of us all—in a place 'prepared of God.' We are not careful to gainsay the fact, that for many women it means a giving up of much that is most dear, both on the part of those who go and those who let them go ; but to give is more blessed than to receive ; and to give up for Him, Who gave up all for us, is to have, if His Word be true, a hundredfold more in this present time, and in the age to come Eternal Life.

THE ARCHBISHOP OF YORK, in closing the meeting, said—I observe from the programme that some concluding words are expected from the chairman ; but, after all that you have heard this morning, what need I say and what can I say ? But at least I feel that I may give expression on your part and on my own to the deep thankfulness with which we have listened to the words addressed to us by our fathers in God from different parts of the Mission-field, and not least for those noble and inspiriting words to which we have just listened from the Bishop of Grahamstown, for indeed in his speech he has rightly gathered up the deepest teachings and the true meaning of such a meeting as this. It is the heartfelt devotion of individual souls that our Lord needs, under whatever circumstances His call may come to us ; and, therefore, I trust that you will allow me also to express in your name and in my own our devout gratitude to the great Head of the Church for all the blessings that He has given to the exertions of our Bishops and priests and deacons and laymen, and, not least, laywomen in all parts of the Mission-field, and for the promise of still greater blessing that He indicates to us in the fruits which we have already been allowed to gather. And one word more. Surely I may express again in your name, as in my own, our deepened sense for this morning's proceedings of our own happy obligation to be more earnest and more fruitful and more self-denying in our support of the great missionary work of the Church ; and, even more than all this, to be more real and more constant in our intercession on behalf of that work and of those whom God has called to labour in it. The obligation of intercession for Missions is one that is readily enough acknowledged. How far is it consistently and really practised ? Surely we shall all strive to be more earnest in uniting our supplications on behalf of the work of the Mission-field with those who have passed away, and in the nearer presence of the Great Head of the Church are praying more earnestly than ever they could pray on earth, and thus the results of our meeting to-day will be, not a mere quickened excitement of missionary sympathy for the moment, but a deepened feeling of the joy as well as of the responsibility of taking part in this blessed work of extending the kingdom of our Lord and Saviour Jesus Christ.

The Benediction was then pronounced by his Grace, and the proceedings terminated.

AFTERNOON MEETING, JUNE 25

THE afternoon meeting began at half-past two. The chair was taken by the Archbishop of Canterbury. The hymn, 'Saviour, sprinkle many nations,' was sung, and prayer was again offered by the Secretary.

THE PRIMATE'S ADDRESS

THE ARCHBISHOP OF CANTERBURY, on rising to address the meeting, was received with hearty cheering. He said—This is the 196th anniversary of this most important Society, and the meeting at this time has a peculiar character, because it is impossible to dissociate the work of this Society and the recollection of all that it has done during the reign of her Majesty from an enthusiastic expression of loyalty to that Queen who has for sixty years reigned over us in the spirit of Christianity, showing at every moment the deep sympathy that she feels with all her people in all that concerns them—a sympathy which is uttered on every occasion when anything whatever may call for sympathy, whether it be great distress and great suffering, or whether it be an occasion of rejoicing. It is impossible for us not to have these things fully in our minds at the present moment. Three days ago we saw the great procession which was intended to express to the Queen and to the whole world the deep loyalty of the English people and the gratitude which we all feel to Almighty God for that which He has done for us during these last sixty years. And of all that went on in that procession I think we may say that the most striking thing was the absolute sincerity and the thorough genuineness of the feelings that were then expressed. There can be no question on the part of any one who saw it or took any part in it that all were animated from their very hearts with the same feeling; that all alike were expressing, not some thing which they merely put on for the moment, but were pouring forth feelings of the deepest and truest earnestness because of what the Queen had been to us, and because of all that God had done for us. And at this time we cannot but still think of the same things. We think of the many blessings that have been slowly but steadily accumulated upon us during the present reign, blessings all of them marked with the characteristic which specially belongs to the blessings that come straight from God; all of them marked by the most wonderful drawing of the people together. There has been no sixty years, in all the time that England has been a nation, of which it could be said that there was so visible a warmth of united affection for one another and so strong a desire to be drawn closer and closer together by every bond of union that could possibly be created. There has been no other time in which men of all classes have felt so deep a sympathy with one another. There has been no time in which from the highest to the lowest, from the Legislature of the whole Empire to the humblest subject of her Majesty, there was a warmer desire for the general good and for blessings immeasurable to be given to all that could possibly share them. And we owe so much of that to the Queen herself because she is the leader in all this sympathy, the very expression of it in almost everything that she ever says or does, and the centre round which all this is stirring. We feel that she does indeed represent the Empire at the head of which she sits. We feel that she is in the very truest sense English to the very core, that she is an Englishwoman and an English Christian. We feel that when she speaks she utters the united voice of all our millions, and we feel that in her heart and in her thoughts there is always stirring that affection which marks all her utterances. And all this has been given to us through her means and around her throne by the providence of our heavenly Father. And in the midst of all this we cannot help observing that one of the things that will mark this reign for all posterity is the spread of the gospel of Christ over all the world. The feeling which draws all Englishmen and all subjects of the Queen together, the feeling of unity which permeates the people of the whole Empire, shows itself in the strong desire that we may all join before the throne of God in the worship of our Saviour and Redeemer ; and long will it be remembered that in this wonderful reign the Church has spread with even more rapidity than the power of the country, and that now we can present to the view of all the world a Church that is really beginning to wake to her great duty and really beginning to be stirred through and through with the noble, and at the same time Christian, desire that all others shall be Christians as we are Christians. This Society has taken a part in the great work, in some respects the leading part, but in all respects a hearty and devoted part ; and it is good that now, when we are looking back upon all the other blessings, we should have clearly before us this blessing which not only is a blessing, but a call to more earnest efforts in the discharge of the great task which the Lord has put upon His Church. We are called by the past ; we are called by that which we have received from God ; we are called by the blessing with which He has blessed all our labours ; and woe be to us if we are deaf to the call. But I think that we shall not be deaf to it, and I hope that this very year, amidst all the other things that it ought to do for Englishmen, will stir the very souls of English people throughout the island, and will stir all men who love the Lord to recognize that He is now reminding us of the duty which belongs to us. There have been times when the Church has done little for the propagation of the Gospel. There have been times when it seemed as if all this work lay outside the ordinary duty of ordinary Christians, as if a man might live a Christian life and be totally indifferent to that which the Church in which he is baptized is pledged to do. It seems that there have been times when men looked upon this as something altogether extraneous, a sort of addition to the Christian life, something which might be taken up by those who happened to have their interest aroused in what was going on in foreign countries. But I trust that we are gradually awaking, and that this year will awake us more than ever before, to the fact, which I cannot think is sufficiently present in the ordinary lives of Christian people, that the Holy Catholic Church lives by the communion of saints, and that that communion of saints is a perpetual demand upon us to make the doctrine and the faith of the Church of God known throughout the world wherever men are to be found. I hope that the time is coming when it will be felt that a man who was indifferent to that object was leaving out one of the most important parts of his Christian life, and therefore crippling it. There can be no question of the imperative character of the duty, but we are all of us slow to be stirred even by the most imperative duties ; and, as it seems to me, we do not yet rise to the height of the position which we hold as a Christian Church, and do not yet accept the task which the Lord put upon us when He told His disciples that they were to go and preach the Gospel to all nations. I hope that, as this great year commemorates and will commemorate through all future time the sympathy which runs through all our people, it will also commemorate the rising of the Church of England to a more thorough appreciation of the call, and that this Society may take her share in doing what the whole Church has to do.

THE CHURCH OF ENGLAND IN THE DOMINION OF CANADA

BY THE MOST REV. THE LORD ARCHBISHOP OF RUPERT'S LAND

THIS paper is intended to bring before you the progress of the Church in Canada since the last Lambeth Conference.

It is a bold undertaking to attempt to compress within fifteen minutes a review of the progress of twenty Dioceses, not a few of which have been advancing relatively in a way peculiar to our young colonies. In addition, something must be said of the new organization of the Church in Canada established in 1893.

The late revered Metropolitan of Canada, the Bishop of Fredericton, in 1888 felt the task of reviewing even the nine Dioceses of the Ecclesiastical Province of Canada so impossible, that he confined himself to his own Diocese. Perhaps that would have been for myself on this occasion the wiser and more useful course. At the best my remarks must be very general and fragmentary, as I have not only not the time, but not the sufficiently definite and accurate information to enter into details.

The Church in the Dominion of Canada consists of the old Ecclesi-

THE LORD ARCHBISHOP OF RUPERT'S LAND 59

astical Province of Canada, with ten Dioceses, under the Archbishop of Ontario as Metropolitan; of the Ecclesiastical Province of Rupert's Land, with eight Dioceses, under the Archbishop of Rupert's Land as Metropolitan; and of the three Dioceses in British Columbia, Columbia, New Westminster, and Caledonia, not yet formed into a province, and over which the Archbishop of Canterbury still acts as Metropolitan. All of these twenty-one Dioceses, with the exception of the Diocese of Caledonia, are now members of the Church of England in the Dominion of Canada, which is governed by a general synod, and is presided over by a Primate, styled the Primate of All Canada.

During the past nine years the Episcopate has been strengthened by the formation of the Diocese of Ottawa in the Province of Canada, out of the Diocese of Ontario; and the Diocese of Selkirk in the Province of Rupert's Land, out of the Diocese of McKenzie River.

The number of Bishops may seem large for a population only about equal to that of Scotland, and of which only a small proportion—not one-fifth—belongs to the Church of England; but in fact a large extent of area creates the same difficulty in superintendence as a crowded population, and with us the presence of the Bishop in every parish—aye, sometimes in every out-station—is hoped for almost yearly. There is, then, somewhat the same feeling in Canada as in England of the need for the well-being of the Church of an even further division of Dioceses. For example, in my own Diocese there are only about 80 clergymen in actual charge of parishes, but many of them have as large a field of work as a whole English county, or say the Diocese of Sodor and Man, and the work which I have, as Bishop, is just as if an English Bishop had to hold a visitation or confirmations one week in Devonshire and the next in Inverness-shire. There are over 200 congregations. The marvellous network of railways in the southern half of Manitoba, a territory nearly as large as England, to which we owe one of our chief difficulties, the extraordinary dispersion of our small immigrant population, enables me, indeed, to cover a large extent of country in a day. Still, the greater part of my Diocese—the northern half of Manitoba, and a vast tract in Ontario, nearly as large as Great Britain—remains a wild, rocky, and wooded wilderness, with a most scanty and scattered Indian population, only to be reached after a journey of several days by boat or canoe, or a very tedious, expensive, and lengthy land journey. It would be easier in time and money to go to St. Petersburg than to some of these Missions.

Bishoprics with us do not require 75,000*l*. and a palace for their foundation; but they should have at least $50,000 or 10,000*l*. Indeed, they should have more, for from the great fall of interest 10,000*l*. means, to-day in Canada, something very different from what it did even 30 years ago.

It is, however, far more difficult to get this 10,000*l*. in Canada than the larger sum in England—indeed, the existing bishopric endowments in Canada, except my own, have been some of them wholly—I believe all of them largely—obtained in England. In the past nine years the endowment of the Bishopric of Niagara has been completed to $75,000, and endowments of at least $50,000 have been raised for Ottawa and Algoma—these endowments mainly in Canada; also the endowment of Qu'Appelle has been raised in England. The Bishopric of Selkirk, like the other bishoprics in purely Indian territory, is supported by the C.M.S., a Society that spent last year on its Indian Missions in the Ecclesiastical Province of Rupert's Land and in British Columbia nearly 20,000*l*.

As regards pressing needs in the Episcopate, the completion of the endowment of the see of Calgary in the Province of Rupert's Land is a matter of anxiety—only 3,000*l*. has yet been raised. If assistance were given, it would be met by important grants from the S.P.C.K. and the Colonial Bishoprics Fund, as well as from this Society. The endowment of the Bishopric of New Westminster is at present to a great extent unproductive. It is very important that some effort should be made to improve its position. It is greatly to be regretted that this bishopric should be crippled at the present juncture, when the population is being so largely increased from the opening of valuable mines.

The number of clergy has increased, I believe, in every Diocese—in some very considerably—but I have not the means of stating accurately the proportion. As might be expected, the increase is most marked in my own Province of Rupert's Land. In my own Diocese the number has risen from fifty-one to eighty-three, and has been doubled in each of the Dioceses of Calgary, Qu'Appelle, and Saskatchewan, and probably Algoma. But the advance in spiritual work, or at any rate in what may be taken as the outward evidences of it, such as in the number of communicants, in the number of those confirmed, in the funds raised for Missions, and in organizations for Church work, is generally very much more marked than in the increase of clergy.

As an example, in the Diocese of Fredericton the number of communicants has increased 25 per cent. on the number of members. In the united Diocese of Ontario, while the whole number of members increased 25 per cent., the number of communicants increased 33 per cent. But, above all, there has been a very great extension in organizations of all kinds for Church work. The Women's Auxiliary is forming branches over the whole Church, and is doing a great deal to create a living interest in Missions, and to bring out gifts of money as well as a great deal of work both for ecclesiastical and charitable uses. Of late years branches of the St. Andrew's Brotherhood have been established in many parishes, and as the membership is usually confined to men of consecrated lives for Christ and much zeal, they are found most helpful in drawing young men within the influences of religion.

The progress of the Domestic and Foreign Missionary Society of the Province of Canada is very encouraging. In 1888 the report gives $15,141 for Domestic Missions, that is, Missions in Algoma and the north-west of Canada, and of $12,417 for Foreign Missions. Last year the corresponding sums were $26,065 for Domestic, and $17,725 for Foreign—an increase in all of $16,292, or nearly 59 per cent.

The sums mentioned include amounts not raised directly by the Mission Board, but only reported to it. This reporting seems to be only partially done. The probability is that, if all sums raised for Missions in the Province of Canada were included, the result would be even more satisfactory.

At the same time, I believe, more is being raised in every Diocese for its own local needs, though there seems much complaint in some of the Dioceses of the Province of Canada that the advance in this does not correspond to the increased amounts for outside Missions, and is not at all equal to the local needs. There have been serious deficiencies in meeting the expenditure for local Missions in several Dioceses. A few facts will show the great financial progress in my own Diocese. The amount reported in 1880 as raised for all purposes was $6,300, last year it was $66,067. The amount raised in 1888 for our local Diocesan Mission Fund was $1,629, and last year $5,358.

The Church in Canada owes its life and growth to the Church Societies in England. Each has been so kind according to its means that I do not like to particularise. The S.P.G., the C.M.S., the S.P.C.K., the C.C.C.S., the Colonial Bishoprics Fund, and, in a less degree, the Bible Society, have in their several spheres of operation done us invaluable service. And the Church in Canada fully and gratefully appreciates and recognizes this weight of obligation. Anyone who suggests the contrary entirely misapprehends the mind of the Canadian Church. But, though we owe so much to other Societies, no doubt the establishing of the Church among the new settlers has been mainly owing to the long continued and generous support of this Society. It has at length withdrawn from several Dioceses, but even last year it still voted to Canada over 13,000*l.* But it has enunciated a policy of rapid reduction and early withdrawal. This policy should have careful consideration. It is felt in Canada that the future progress of the Church—indeed almost its existence in some parts of the Dominion —is put in jeopardy by it. Canada is a young colony of large resources. From a civil point of view it is very capable. Even Manitoba, young as it is, with its generous, vigorous people, could support all its means of grace but for our divided Christianity, and, if we hold our hand, others will make it a Christian land. But, unfortunately, the Church people in Manitoba are not, I fear, over a fifth of the population—at any rate not a fourth—and so scattered is the small handful of 200,000, the whole population of Manitoba, over the vast territory as large as England which is receiving settlers, that last year out of 786 school districts 740 schools had not an average attendance of 30 children, 640 had not an average of 20, 462 had not an average of 15, and 211 schools not of 10 ; and the children of our Church people, on an average, would only form a third to a sixth of these. That is the state of things that the Church has to meet ; yet for a full and convenient supply of the means of Grace there should almost be a church for every school, and in a majority of cases each of these little centres of population in that fertile land is the nucleus of what may be expected to be a considerable, helpful settlement at no distant day. It will be a sorry retrospect for the Church if these new settlements are starved by it. The history of the progress of the Church in my Diocese in the past 17 years —in a great measure from the generous aid of this Society—tells what may be expected if this aid is not prematurely curtailed. In 1880 there were only six Missions for new settlers ; in 1897, though fourteen parishes with twenty clergy have become self-supporting and are liberally contributing to our Mission funds, we are supporting fifty-five Missions for settlers. Of these fifteen are unfortunately still without resident clergymen, though almost each of them is ready to give 50*l*. to 80*l*. towards a missionary.

I believe there is not a Mission in my Diocese with a village in it having 200 Church people—including men, women, and children—which is not self-supporting and helping our Missions. The reduction of the Society's grants means in my Diocese the crippling of our work and the stoppage of progress, but in the more western Dioceses of Qu'Appelle and Calgary and, I fear, New Westminster, it means the closing of nearly half the Missions. There is no ground for supposing that any appreciably greater help will for some time come from Eastern Canada. And our needs may greatly increase. It is quite possible that a considerable influx of people may be brought by the mines being opened in the Ontario part of my Diocese, in New Westminster, and even at the Youcon, in the diocese of Selkirk.

It is true that the Church in Canada has been consolidated in one body, but it will evidently be some time before there will be much practical result from the consolidation. The consolidated Church is governed by a general synod, a representative body after the usual form in the colonies. There is an Upper House of twenty Bishops, and a Lower House consisting of clerical and lay representatives elected by the diocesan synods. Nothing can be done in the Church unless with the separate consent of Bishops, clergy, and laity. At our last meeting in Winnipeg some important measures were passed, particularly a scheme for missionary work and a Canon for a final court of appeal. But the scheme for missionary work is encountering obstacles, and will not apparently amount to anything, at least till after the next meeting of the Provincial Synod of the Province of Canada. Time does not allow me to say more respecting the consolidation of the Church, except this, that it has been entered on as a very natural and helpful combination in a country already united civilly. It did not mean any independence of the Mother Church more than was already forced by circumstances on the Provinces of Canada and Rupert's Land, and it was very far from our minds to give by it any intimation that the Church in Canada was now able to walk alone, although we fondly hoped it might in time help towards that desirable end. Indeed, for myself nothing would give me greater joy than to see the reduction of English grants proceeding steadily, if I thought this practicable without grievous loss to the Church.

DOMESTIC MISSIONS OF THE CHURCH OF THE UNITED STATES

BY THE LORD BISHOP OF MISSOURI

OUT of the very *Partibus Transmarinis* indicated in the Seal of the Venerable Society I come to discharge my duty of this day. That duty is to speak of the Domestic Missions of our American Church of the United States.

Home, to a citizen, is where the flag of his country flies. Hence, to us, Domestic Missions, or Home Missions, are those promoted by our American Church within the area of the United States; and Foreign Missions, those carried on in countries outside of the jurisdiction of the United States. In a large sense, Home Missions may be accounted the work of Church Extension; and Foreign Missions the special, blessed effort to accomplish the evangelization of the heathen world. Yet, in a small way, we do something in Greece, and Haiti, and Cuba, and Brazil, and Mexico which cannot be classified under Missions to heathen. And, on the other hand, we have in our own country some heathen Chinese and not a few heathen aboriginal Indians among whom we are doing some evangelizing work. But, in the main, our preaching of the Gospel to the heathen is done in China, and Japan, and Africa, under our three Foreign Missionary Bishops resident respectively in those countries. We are glad to do it. We are sorry we are not doing more. And the main work of Domestic Missions is to extend our Church in out-reach and numbers, in influence and strength, upon our own soil.

Technically, there is a further definitive meaning to our term, Domestic Missions. Every Bishop in his own field, by himself, or in connection with a Diocesan Missionary Society, is busy in getting money and placing men for the upbuilding of the Church in that field. Moreover, every rector of a parish and pastor of a flock may be well interested, and some of them are earnestly so, in extending the sway of the Church to souls not yet brought in, and in regions round about. These are Home Missions of the best and truest sort. But we do not include them under the term Domestic Missions. This term we confine to the work in the home field done by the American Church as a whole.

Triennially all our Bishops, and clerical representatives and lay representatives elected by the Dioceses, meet in General Convention. With us this General Convention is the supreme governing body of the Church. Its Triennial Session continues usually for nearly a month; and on the third day it resolves itself into a 'Board of Missions,' and continues in such session for such period of time as may be necessary to consider, and direct, to provide for and promote the Foreign Missions and the Domestic Missions of the Church. Between the Triennial Sessions a representative 'Missionary Council,' meeting annually, and an executive 'Board of Managers,' of constant authority, exercise the power of the 'Board of Missions' in consideration and direction of missionary work. Into the less strong Dioceses, and into the Missionary Districts not yet having attained to the self-support and autonomy of Dioceses this 'Board of Missions' enters for its helpful work of Domestic Missions; but always in counsel and co-operation with the Bishop having jurisdiction. The Board of Missions also provides the salaries of the Missionary Bishops having charge of the Missionary Districts.

Just now the Board is giving stipends, larger or smaller, to 261 missionaries in 35 Dioceses, and to 122 more in 19 Missionary Districts, besides meeting the salaries of 14 Missionary Bishops. By the last year's report the Board received from gifts of the faithful $395,297.50, or about £81,000, for the work of Domestic Missions. Designated gifts are used as directed, undesignated gifts to Missions are divided equally between Domestic and Foreign.

Suffer a few more statistics. The area of the United States includes 45 States, 3 organized Territories (Arizona, New Mexico, and Oklahoma), and 2 unorganized Territories (Alaska and Indian Territory). We have 58 Dioceses. Many a State has more than one Diocese in it. New York has five. Some States are as yet only Missionary Districts, and some Missionary Districts have been carved out of Dioceses which were immense in extent but feeble in Church strength. Texas and California are instances. We have 58 Diocesan Bishops, 6 Bishops Coadjutor, 14 Domestic Missionary Bishops, 3 Foreign Missionary Bishops, and 3 retired Bishops—84 in all. Three Domestic Missionary Bishoprics are vacant, though the Districts have Episcopal care under the direction of the presiding Bishop; and two Missionary Districts, though established by Canon, remain under the charge, respectively, of the Bishops a part of whose field they made before organization.

Domestic Missions then, with us, is the name given to the effort of our American Church in a united way and on national lines to make Churchmen of our American people. The work calls for much faith and zeal. Eight leading denominations provide the most of the religious teaching for our people. I name them in the order of the number of their respective communicants: The Roman Catholics, the Methodists, the Baptists, the Presbyterians, the Lutherans, the Disciples of Christ, our own Church, and the Congregationalists. Of the 3,700,000 Baptists 1,300,000 are negroes; and of the 4,600,000 Methodists, 1,000,000 are negroes.

It is observed that we are next to the foot of the list. We seem as 'the conies a feeble folk,' but in humble confidence we claim that our house, like theirs, is made 'in the rocks.' We hold, we venture to feel sure, for ourselves and in trust for all our American countrymen, three things of invaluable worth: Catholic Dogma, Apostolic Order, Historic Succession. And at the door of our rock-hewn house, in assertion and protection of our home-given ecclesiastical rights, we stand in calm, but firm and unyielding protest against all foreign episcopal usurpation. Loving all who love the Lord Jesus Christ in sincerity, we mean, God helping us, to hold fast our trust. And without bitterness in our protest, and making much allowance in our mind for the stern necessity of the logic of events, we accord willing honour to a venerated brother for his goodness of heart, but waive off unhesitatingly the outstretched hands of Italian episcopal regimen.

In the United States there are 143 distinct religious denominations. There are 17 kinds of Methodists, and 16 kinds of Lutherans, 13 kinds of Baptists, and 12 kinds of Presbyterians. Alas, for the schism fever and the sect habit when they run riot! In my Diocese, as a friend lately recounted to me, there is a congregation of one of these 143 denominations. One tenet is the washing of the disciples' feet. A subjective rationalist among the members submitted that the Scriptural practice would be adequately followed if one foot only were washed. The orthodox traditionists insisted that the two must be washed. The objector and his admirers withdrew. The severed congregations became known to the profane as the 'one-foot Church' and the 'two-foot Church.'

One sees at a glance that our love for all believers must be linked fast with undying loyalty to the Church. Steadiness of faith, warmth of zeal, vigour of work must go with the aim to mould our American people into Churchmen. That aim, if we keep to it in a loving way, the Holy Ghost, the real Vicar on earth of the Lord Jesus Christ, will surely bless. And, spite of the craze of sectism, there is an American common sense, own daughter of Anglo-Saxon practical sense, working in the breast of our countrymen for unity. The very existence of one of our sects is proof of this out-reaching, in a blind way, after unity. The 'Disciples of Christ' number 650,000 communicants. In my own Diocese they outnumber Churchmen 8 to 1, and have 500 ministers to our 50 clergymen. They are immersionists and antipædobaptists. They are less than one hundred years old. They are sometimes called 'Campbellites' from Alexander Campbell, their founder, or their first distinguished leader. They call themselves the 'Christian Church' and claim that there should be no other creed or charter for the Church proposed than 'the apostles' doctrine and fellowship and breaking of bread and prayers.' In a subjective, haphazard sort of fashion they are groping for the Christian Church of Antioch, and, throwing overboard historic sense and historic authority, are stumbling to their fall over the Catholic Church of the centuries. 'Speaking the truth in love,' it ought to be ours, as God shows us the way, to enlighten them and win them to loyalty —to the substance, where they are wandering after the shadow.

Parishes, Dioceses, and the Board of Missions have big work to do to promote Home Missions in the United States. Is it noticed that out of our 58 Dioceses the Board sends help into more than half—35? It is a helping of the weaker by the strong. May the blessed work go on!

We are not discouraged. In 1835 we made our first Missionary Bishop, Jackson Kemper. So we put in practice what it had taken our American Church 51 years to learn, and what it took the Church of England 180 years to learn, that to send a bishop at the head and in the lead is the true way to do missionary work. In 1835 we had 16 bishops, 763 clergy, and 36,000 communicants. In 1897 we have 84 bishops, 4,618 clergymen, and 636,000 communicants. An increase of bishops fivefold, ot clergy sixfold, and of communicants seventeenfold. The population of the United States in 1830 was 12,866,000; in 1890, 62,480,000; an increase of less than fivefold. In 1835 there was one communicant of the Church to every 353 of the population. To-day there is one to every 98. We thank God and take courage.

In closing let thanks be said, too, to the venerable Society. Our forefathers in America called aloud 'Transiens adjuva nos.' The Society responded. It tried to send bishops. Complications of Ministers of State and unrelenting oppositions of dissenters prevented. But it sent godly and well-learned missionaries. Seventy-seven of them were at work in the American colonies when the Revolution broke out. Nor has the venerable Society stayed its generous hand since. It sent me a grant when I was Missionary Bishop of Utah to help me build a Church among the Mormons. As the chronicler of our Domestic Missions, as a representative of American Churchmen, and as a Missionary Bishop helped by her beneficent bounty, I beg to say to her this day warm and unforgetting thanks.

THE FOREIGN MISSIONS OF THE CHURCH OF THE UNITED STATES

BY THE LORD BISHOP OF KENTUCKY

I COUNT myself happy, Mr. President, my Lords and gentlemen, that I am the spokesman of the Church in the United States of America upon this most auspicious occasion. It is meet and right that a Church which owes under God almost its very existence to the nourishing care of this venerable Society, shall bring to its foster mother a report of its doings in the long years which have passed since, in the good providence of God, that fostering care was withdrawn and her independent life began. It is a special privilege that we English-speaking men, the sons of England's Church, shall come to add our thanksgivings to yours for the glorious continuance of a glorious reign, because the period of our Foreign Missionary enterprise synchronises almost exactly with that of her gracious Majesty's rule. For us Americans too, then, the Victorian era affords ground for thanksgiving and praise, because in it our branch of the Catholic Church of English-speaking people has aroused to a realization of her Christ-given embassage to the world.

You will readily understand without any words of mine that the condition of the Church in the United States of America when the long war was ended, when the infant nation was but newly born, was not such as to make possible the essaying of missionary endeavour.

A handful of congregations they were, these Churchmen, scattered along the great Atlantic coast. They had no Bishop, and had never seen one. Nominally they had been under the jurisdiction of the Lord Bishop of London, three thousand miles away, but their clergy had never known a father in God, and of the laity but few had ever received the seal of confirmation. Ignorant practically of ecclesiastical procedure, their horizon was bounded by congregational necessity, and their utmost of known activity was the election of vestrymen and churchwardens. The supreme question then presenting itself to their wisest men, clergy and laity alike, was how to keep alive the ancient Church of their love. The difficulty of securing Bishops seemed well-nigh insuperable, the technical difficulties presented by England's law being aggravated by the hostility of the Nonconformists at home; and the large part of the clergy who had served the Colonial Church had departed with the old Government. Pardon me, I do not mean to recite the story of the struggling Church in the United States. But I must mention these items of the missionary account as explanation of the slow beginning and of the long-time little progress. The Church must provide for the continuance of her own life before she could begin the God-given work of imparting that life to others. And further, when her organization had been completed, when the English succession had been given us, in addition to that already received from the persecuted remainder of the ancient Church of Scotland, when synods had begun to assemble with Bishops over them, and the federation of dioceses to gather its representatives to legislate for the common good, what place could then be found in the deliberations of any Council, or in the thought of any man's heart, for Foreign Missions? Foreign Missions? Why, the whole vast continent is ours to evangelize! The red man is being pushed further and further to the setting sun, and the slave-trader is bringing other barbarians to crowd our settled lands; what room for thought of Missions more foreign, than to these heathen of America and of Africa, at our very doors? I am old enough to have heard this same cry of almost remonstrance against foreign missionary effort. I can remember to have heard in a Council of our Church, from one who was then among its leaders, 'Let the Church of England, the powerful, the long-established, whose island home is cared for by her thousands of priests, let her do all the foreign missionary work; there is obligation resting upon us to carry the Ancient Church and the Ancient Creeds to the teeming population of our own continent and we may not diminish our puny missionary resources by thus in sentimental folly distributing them to all the quarters of the globe.' We may hardly be surprised that men so thought and so spake. And yet the Church in the United States had hardly more than attained its majority before other voices than these were heard, before there did arise of her sons men who, like the great Apostle, could not be persuaded by all the entreaty of the need at home that they should not adventure themselves into privation and danger for the Gospel's sake.

As early as 1814 there came a clarion call from him who was then the Bishop of nearly the whole of New England, that churchmen remember 'the indispensable duty and most benevolent work in all Christians to impart to mankind the knowledge and the means of salvation.'

Two years thereafter we hear of a young man called Andrus—*sit nomen omen*—a candidate for Holy Orders in this same diocese, offering himself to the Church Missionary Society of England for missionary service. The offer was declined, with the wise suggestion from the Committee 'that the most effectual way of raising the missionary zeal in America would be the formation of a Church Missionary Society in the Episcopal Church of the United States.' Straightway local Missionary Societies were formed in some of the dioceses, notably in that of Pennsylvania, but not until the meeting of the General Convention of the Church, in 1820, were steps taken toward the formation of a General Missionary Society, and in the following year its constitution was adopted. It will suffice to say of it that it followed the examples of the great Societies in England, and that its membership was restricted to the members of the General Convention of the Church and such other persons as should make regular contribution to its treasury. And so the work was begun. It may not be uninteresting that I add that Mr. Andrus—the Andrews of our Missionary body—impatient of delay, went in this same year to Sierra Leone and the Bassa country as an agent of the American Colonization Society, and there laid down his life, the forerunner of the goodly company of our heroes who there rest in the missionary's grave.

It is interesting to note that the first selected Foreign Mission was in West Africa, and that as early as 1822 a man and his wife were appointed to go thither as catechists and teachers. But these persons apparently never left America, and the first Mission established was that to the aborigines in the western part of our own land. Then Missions to the Indians were considered, and were called Foreign Missions. Now I am thankful to say, through the devoted labours of the Bishop of Minnesota, the apostle of the Indians, and of the no less devoted Bishop of South Dakotah, in whose charge they chiefly lie, no Missions are more domestic, more at home with us, than Indian Missions, and therefore are beyond the scope of this Paper.

For fifteen years after its organization this General Missionary Society, it might almost be said by the superficial observer, accomplished nothing. Its executive committee met regularly, nor was there lack of interest in the men who then directed the Society's action. Agents were sent out to instruct the people as to the need, the opportunity, the obligation. Reports were made to the triennial synods of the Church, in which we read of plans formed and frustrated, of want of missionaries and want of funds. But despite the appearance to the contrary, much was being accomplished. In 1829, doubtless because of the sympathy of our countrymen with the sufferings of the Greeks, the Society sent out a clergyman of the Church to be a missionary to these people, whom the Committee described as 'descended from an ancient and Apostolic branch of the Church of Christ, but among whom, being without the Holy Scriptures and destitute of education, a corrupt form of Christianity prevails, except where even this has given place to infidelity.' Let me not fail to add that the venerable Bishop of Pennsylvania, the

President of the Society, in his letter of instruction to the missionary, bids him present to any Bishop of the Greek Church whom he may meet, 'the profound respect and paternal affection of a brother Bishop, in the forty-second year of his episcopacy,' and states that 'he recognizes the Greek Church as of Apostolic origin, and a sister of the Church in which he (the writer) unworthily holds a conspicuous station.' Such was the first actual beginning of our foreign missionary work, the establishment of a school at Athens, which still lives, and which has educated, with the approval of the Greek Archbishop there, a great number of the mothers of the men who are to-day valiantly resisting the oppressive power of the Moslem.

But more than this was done in these fifteen years. Although but little money was collected, although but one Mission was planted, and that not in a heathen land, yet our own people were educated to the point of remedying the inherent deficiency in our system, and of declaring, as was done in 1835, that the Church herself is the great Missionary Society, and that by his baptism into the Divine Name every Christian is made a member of it, and as such is bound by baptismal vow to bear his part in this the one peculiar service enjoined by the Lord. I speak with all deference. I recognise with gratitude and with thankfulness the splendid work accomplished for us in America long ago, and for the millions in other lands to-day, by this venerable Society and her honoured sisters, as voluntary societies ; but for us in America I have to tell that the very beginning of our efficiency as a Missionary Church was this recognition of universal individual responsibility, and this declaration of the all-inclusive membership of our Missionary Society.

On Christmas Day, 1836, our first Missionary to the heathen, the Rev. Dr. Savage, landed at Cape Palmas, West Africa, and on the 4th July following came Payne and Minor to join him. There Minor sleeps, having speedily succumbed to the dreadful fever ; but Payne came home in 1851 to be consecrated the first Bishop of Cape Palmas, and resigned only in 1870. Thus he wrote in his last report, 'For myself I fear that little ability remains to aid directly this glorious work. Thirty-three years connection with one of the most unhealthy portions of the globe has left me the mere wreck of a man. But I claim that in devoting myself to preaching among the Gentiles the unsearchable riches of Christ, I was no fool. On the contrary, I did obey literally the command of my Lord. I did follow in the very footsteps of Apostles, martyrs and prophets. . . . And now God has demonstrated in my own person what I have always maintained : that the Christian Missionary, as well as the dealers in slaves, ivory, and tobacco, can live and have His work prosper in Africa.'

To-day we have in Africa the Bishop Ferguson, a coloured man, fourteen clergymen, eleven candidates for Holy Orders, five postulants, twenty-one lay readers, eleven hundred and twelve communicants, forty teachers, and two business agents ; with property valued at $46,000.

The next year, 1837, came Boone to China. Tradition tells that as he walked the floor of his room in the Theological Seminary talking to his room-mate of his desire and purpose to go to China, he was told that his purpose was chimerical, that there was no door open for him. The reply came quick, the expression of the spirit that must conquer, 'If by going to China and working there for the term of my natural life, I could but *oil the hinges* of the door, so that those who come after could enter and work there, gladly would I go.' For a long time after his arrival he was not permitted to preach, but patiently he toiled on awaiting the opening of the door, and in 1847 he baptized his first convert. He died full of years and of honours, as the first missionary Bishop, to be succeeded after a number of years by his own son. To-day we have in China a Bishop in charge, six foreign and five native presbyters, two foreign and twenty native deacons, one foreign and seven native candidates for Holy Orders, physicians, nurses, teachers, catechists, and assistants, one hundred and five ; ten hundred and twenty-four communicants, with churches, a college, a medical school, hospitals and schools, of an estimated value of $223,000.

And I may not fail to add that the Bishop who immediately preceded the present occupant of the See, with a body paralysed, yet dwells by choice among the people to whom he went with the glad tidings, and labours diligently to perfect the translation he has made of the whole Bible into the Mandarin dialect.

In Japan ours was the first modern Mission established. Two men in Holy Orders landed at Nagasaki, from China, in 1859. One soon retired from ill-health, the other lived to become the first Bishop of the Mission in 1866. But not until 1868 could aggressive missionary work be undertaken, and not until 1888 were Japanese subjects constitutionally allowed freedom of religious belief. One man was baptized in 1866, another in 1872, and another in 1874. To-day there are in our Mission in Japan, the Bishop, the retired Bishop, the saintly Williams, the founder of the Mission, thirteen foreign and seven native presbyters, one foreign and eight native deacons, fifteen candidates for Holy Orders, eleven postulants for Holy Orders, twenty-five foreign teachers and workers, fifty-five native catechists, twenty-two native Bible readers, seventy-five native teachers, and thirteen hundred and eighty-three communicants. And we have there property, churches, college, Divinity school, hospitals and school buildings, of an estimated value of $120,000.

Besides, we largely maintain the Church in Haiti, albeit that Church is independent and not a Mission of the Church in the United States. This Church has a Bishop, eight presbyters, three deacons, two postulants for Holy Orders, eighteen lay readers, three teachers, with a property of the estimated value of $30,000.

An attempt was made to be foster-mother to a Protestant Church in our neighbouring Republic of Mexico. The priest chosen by the Synod was duly consecrated to the episcopate by our House of Bishops, upon the basis of a concordat as to doctrine and liturgy and discipline. But alas ! the concordat did bind but one party, and in a little while the affairs of the Mexican Church were so muddled that there remained no course or our Bishops save to suspend the Bishop from the exercise of his office, as his own agreement empowered them to do. The faithful clergy and laity there are now superintended by a priest appointed by our presiding Bishop, reporting to him, and supported from our missionary treasury. Under his direction the work goes on.

And finally in carrying out a plan of the Society formed in 1830, but never acted upon, a most successful Mission has been planted in Brazil, by some devoted men and women, who are maintained by a Society once wholly independent, and now auxiliary to the General Society, whose separate existence is, I think I may say, now maintained only because of the necessity, in order to hold vested funds. This Mission has been placed under the provisional charge of one of our Bishops, and his report of it after visitation was most enthusiastic. From his report and that of the missionaries, they are labouring among men who are heathens, albeit the baptized children of the Church of Rome, and hungry and thirsty they crowd to beg the bread of heaven, the water of life, the pure Word of God, the Sacraments duly administered, which our Church has brought them.

In a word, this hath God wrought. He has made us realise at least in a measure that the Church is the Missionary Society, that every baptized man must take part in this work, and this realisation is ever increasing. Last year eight hundred and thirty-four more parishes than two years ago contributed to Foreign Missions ; and two hundred and twenty-two thousand dollars was received during the year for the work outside of our own country, the largest amount ever received in any one year, and this notwithstanding the fact that the past year has been one of extraordinary financial depression. True this is but a paltry sum as compared with our people's wealth and proverbial lavish expenditure. But compare it with the results of the year ending when your Sovereign Lady was crowned, and it is encouraging. And, please God, the men of the next generation shall not be as those who are now passing away, for our Sunday School children gave to Missions last time seventy thousand dollars.

And the reaction of missionary interest upon the growth of the Church at home has come to us as to you. Until 1835 our Church in the United States hardly held her own. Since that time when she began—really began—her foreign missionary work, the population of the Republic has increased about four and one-half times, and the number of our communicants has increased about sixteen and one-third times. Such the report I have to make. A paltry thing is all our work in comparison with that so much greater of your own Societies ; and yet for it we thank God, and because of it we take courage, and for it we bid you, our mother Society, to thank God, and to be very courageous in your ventures to build up like agents for Christ in your great Colonial Empire.

One word in conclusion. Sirs, we be brethren. How then shall there be rivalry or contention among the missionaries of the one communion and fellowship, in the face of the heathen ? Surely though each as independent, each as accountable to the one Lord, must do her work in her own way, there must be possible a path of unity and of concord, a minimising of the differences due to separated nationality, an emphasising of the greater fact of the unity of the Spirit, nay, of the unity of the Body as well.

This, the greeting of your daughter Church to the mother in her Jubilee year: Come let us run together with gladness, with eager step, with self-effacing sacrifice and labour, that we may 'tell it out among the heathen that the Lord is King.'

From the Diamond of your Jubilee let the fuller light shine forth into the darkness of heathendom, to bring them the knowledge of that God who has saved the Queen.

THE CHURCH'S WORK IN WESTERN AUSTRALIA

BY THE LORD BISHOP OF PERTH

THE object I set before myself in writing this paper is to obtain help from home for the work of the Church in the Diocese of Perth—to obtain help which, I believe, we are justified in asking and have a right to receive. I must show the need for help. It is necessary to do so, because I am told that people say: 'Why does Western Australia require help when it is a country in which gold is obtained?' And at a missionary meeting not long since the deputation spoke of my Diocese as 'one which did not now require help.'

One answer to this statement is to be found in the joint letter of the Australian Bishops, who, knowing the state of the case, most generously put on one side for the time their own needs, to bring before the public the absolute necessity there was for help at the present time in the Diocese of Perth. I regret to say that there has not been that response to this powerful appeal which was anticipated. It is therefore—so it seems to me—necessary that I should endeavour to remove some of the misconceptions which certainly exist with regard to my Diocese.

It is impossible to understand what Church work is like in a colony unless we know something about its geography and history.

Geography.—1. The Diocese of Perth is coterminous with the colony of Western Australia, which extends from 13° 30′ S. lat. to 35° 8′ S. lat., and from Dirk Hartog's Island in 112° 50′ E. long. to 129° E. long. Its greatest length in statute miles is 1,480 from north to south, and its breadth about 1,000 miles from east to west.

The area is a little more than 1,000,000 square miles, and is as large as the following countries in Europe all joined together:

	Square miles
Austro-Hungary	264,443
Great Britain and Ireland	120,840
France	204,092
Germany	208,640
Italy	114,410

								Square miles
Greece	.	.	.	.	.	.	.	24,970
Switzerland	.	.	.	.	.	.	.	15,892
Servia	.	.	.	.	.	.	.	19,050
Montenegro	.	.	.	.	.	.	.	3,486
								975,823

The total amount of coast-line is 3,000 miles.

The climate varies from tropical in the north-west to hot and dry in the middle zone, and to an English summer climate at Albany, and is everywhere very trying to Englishmen at the first.

History.—Australia was discovered about 300 years ago by the Dutch, but it was not until 1688 that the first Englishman, William Dampier, landed on the coast of Western Australia, and not until 141 years afterwards that Captain Fremantle, in 1829, in H.M.S. 'Challenger,' anchored off the Swan River and hoisted the British flag. He was followed soon after by two ships bringing emigrants and a detachment of the 63rd Regiment. With the arrival of these two ships the history of the colony began.

At first, and for many years, the early settlers had very hard times, and felt themselves almost cut off from the world. Fifty years ago there were but 4,000 people in the colony.

In order to help the colony request was made to the home Government that convicts should be sent out. This was done in 1850, on condition that for each convict one free emigrant should also be sent. The result of this was that roads, bridges, &c., were made, and the country was opened out. Convicts continued to be sent out until 1868, when, at the request of the colonists, no more were deported. In all about 10,000 convicts were sent out. You can all understand that the presence of so many convicts would have an effect on the morals of the people, though Western Australia never fell into the immoral condition which we are told came upon some other penal settlements. About six years ago there were 50,000 people in the colony, now there are 160,000. This great increase is entirely due to the finding of gold.

History of the Church.—At first the Church was served by Government chaplains appointed and paid for by the home Government. Ecclesiastically, Western Australia was in the Diocese of Australia until 1847, when it became part of the Diocese of Adelaide. Bishop Short paid two official visits to Western Australia, a record of which is to be found in his life. In 1857 the see of Perth was formed by letters patent, and in 1876 the Imperial Government withdrew their help, and the Diocese was properly organized with a synod and council.

But now the question comes—and I have been asked it over and over again—Why cannot the people themselves pay for the support of their own clergy?

In the first place, it is rather strange that one should be asked this in a country where the munificence of our fathers has provided churches and endowments in every parish in the kingdom. I thought last Sunday, when preaching on behalf of the Jubilee Sustentation Fund of the Clergy, that if we had 100*l.* a year as an endowment for every parish, that I would not ask for another penny from home. But in the next place, just consider what the work of a new clergyman is. I send him to a new goldfields town, which has perhaps been in existence six months. What does he find? About 500 or 1,000 people living in iron houses, or Hessian shanties, or under canvas. There is no church, no school, no parsonage, nothing but a piece of ground given by the Government. At first all he can do is to hold service in any building he can obtain. Then he has to try to build a school, or a church, and a little hut for himself, at the same time obtaining subscriptions towards his own stipend. How can you expect people, many of whom have been neglected and in whose hearts must first of all be stirred up the religious sense, to do all this all at once? The idea is absurd. They must be helped at first, afterwards they will be all right.

Present Position.—When I went out, a little over two years ago, I found a population of 100,000 people cared for by about twenty-five clergy, scattered about from Roebourne in the north-west to Albany in the south, a distance by sea of about 2,000 miles. The parishes or districts were, of course, terribly large, for it was enough to strike terror into the heart of a new comer to contemplate wasting a large amount of time in the getting from one place to another. The Government granted a subsidy of 2,000*l.* a year to the Church, as it did smaller amounts, *pro rata* of Church members, to the Roman Catholics and Wesleyans. Last year this grant was withdrawn. This withdrawal had been expected, and an attempt had been made to provide for the evil day. The Government, however, behaved with great liberality, and gave to the Church as compensation for the annual grant the sum of 20,000*l.* This has been invested, but still a deficit of 800*l.* a year had to be made up, apart altogether from providing money for new work.

This was our first serious difficulty. To a great extent it has been overcome.

Then the next difficulty arose from the influx of people, at one time at the rate of 1,000 a week.

New towns on the goldfields sprang up like magic. Where but a few months before the foot of white man had never trod, a reef would be found and a town of 500 or 1,000 people be formed. Of course, at once a clergyman should have been sent there. And requests without end kept on coming in, 'Please send us a clergyman.' What could I do? We had no money with which to pay any more clergy, and there were no men to send.

After a time we managed to send a few new men, and with splendid results. But what appears to me to be the most lamentable fact is this: that whereas the Wesleyans could apply to their Central Committee and have at least, I should think, twenty new men sent over to them during the last two years, often to occupy the places where we should have been, there is no one person, no body, and no authority, to whom a Bishop of the Church can apply and say, 'Send me twenty men to open out new work in the Church of God, in the time of this my difficulty and opportunity.'

I am not now blaming the Missionary Societies, for I do not know what the Diocese would have done without the generous—most generous—assistance, given for years, of the S.P.G., the S.P.C.K., and the Colonial and Continental Society.

The present position of the Church in the colony is this. We have our Church fully organised, with a synod and a body of trustees incorporated by Act of Parliament. We have thirty-five clergy, and a goodly number of honorary lay readers, without whose help it would be impossible to keep up the services in our scattered parishes, where the clergyman has perhaps six little churches to serve. We have a certain amount of endowment, and we are liberally helped by the S.P.G., S.P.C.K. (in the building of churches), by the Colonial and Continental Society, and by my English committee, whose secretary, Miss Maurice, works very hard. We have power to teach in all State schools.

Our Wants are.—About a dozen men at once, who must be full of the missionary spirit, not coming out for the sake of health only, or because they think that life will be more free and interesting, but who, knowing that the work is hard and the life full of trials, are willing to endure hardness as good soldiers of Jesus Christ for the spreading of the Gospel.

But then, in addition to men, we want money wherewith to pay them, for the people who come to the goldfields come to make money, not because they have it. There is no leisured class. The greater part of the money subscribed in London for the gold mines does not leave London. It certainly does not reach Western Australia. And the vast majority of the men who come over, come by themselves, leaving their wives and families in the other colonies, ready to be sent for if the men think the fields are to be permanent, or if they get on well. The consequence of this is that a large sum (20,000*l.*) is sent away every week to the other colonies to keep the wives and families of the men in Western Australia.

Our next want is a Missionary for the Chinese, of whom there are a large number in the colony. It seems a pity to go to China and neglect the Chinese living on British soil, where the chance of converting them is so much greater.

We want, too, a Missionary to the aliens, especially the Afghans and others who come with the camels. We also require a Missionary who knows, or can soon learn, the language of the aborigines.

Very little has been done for the natives. Now, however, we are just about to start a Mission in the north-west, where the Government has set apart 100,000 acres for this purpose.

We want district nurses. I wish I could find some large-hearted women of means who would work amongst us for a few years.

Then we want either another Diocesan Bishop or an Assistant Bishop. No one who looks at the map of the colony can say that mine is an unreasonable wish. A new Bishop in the goldfields would, I am sure, do an immense amount of good, and I should still have more work than I could do. (The Roman Catholics are going to form two more dioceses, I believe, this year.)

It is a great mistake for the Bishop always to be away from the capital. Yet this is almost my position now, and it is certain to be the case until I can obtain some help. To show you how urgent this is, I may tell you that last year I travelled over 21,000 miles, and this year before I left the Diocese I had travelled 6,000 miles, and still there are many places to which I have not yet been able to find my way. Last year I travelled 1,000 miles there and 1,000 miles back to confirm two candidates.

I am convinced that a goldfields Bishop would do untold good, and in order to prepare the way for such a grand step in advance, I have appointed an Archdeacon at Coolgardie to help me to organise the work.

Perth is so far away from the goldfields, as far as from London to Edinburgh, and travelling is so slow (infinitely better now, though, than two years ago), it is necessary to have someone in authority on the spot.

The first objection which has to be met with regard to the appointment of such a Bishop is this. Will the goldfields be permanent? Well, of course, it is impossible to say for certain, but as far as I can see—and I have been over the fields and down a great many mines, and have spoken to most of the leading men on the spot—there is no doubt about the permanence of the fields; there is plenty of gold. Last year the gold output was 1,000,000*l.*, and this year the Premier tells me it will be over 2,000,000*l.* It only requires energy and perseverance and skill to make Western Australia one of the largest gold-producing countries in the world.

You will see, then, our difficulties :

1. A large territory with a scattered population, making it necessary for the clergy to travel long distances in order to hold services once a month, sometimes once a quarter, in different parts of their districts; one clergyman, for instance, drives 500 miles every month.

2. The rapid increase in the towns. Perth has grown from 15,000 to 30,000 since I went out.

3. The rapid influx of people coming to the goldfields, with new centres of life continually springing up.

4. The want of suitable men—men well educated and full of manliness and zeal, and willing to devote themselves, without fear of man or fever, to the work.

5. Want of means to adequately carry on the work in a country where expenses, such as building and horse keep, are very high indeed.

6. Want of Missionaries for special work among the aborigines, the Chinese, and the aliens from India.

In conclusion, let me express what I believe to be a simple fact—viz., that we have in my Diocese now for the Church of England the very grandest opportunity which has ever been given to her. Half the people before the great influx belonged to us; of those who have lately come very many belong to us and very few are otherwise than well affected towards us. If we only had the men and the means to send a new man to every new place as it was formed, we should retain our own people and gather in numbers of others, who would be only too delighted to come back if they saw us really in earnest.

'There is a tide in the affairs of men which, taken at the flood, leads on to victory.' Such a tide is passing over my Diocese now, and the flood is at its height. Who will come forward at the time of the Church's need to help us to ride upon that flood to victory, for God and the dear old Church of our Fathers?

THE WEST INDIAN PROVINCE

BY THE MOST REV. THE LORD BISHOP OF JAMAICA

I CANNOT accomplish the impossible task of adequately stating in fifteen minutes the facts needing now to be made known respecting the Church in the West Indian Province.

THE PROVINCE GENERALLY.

The ecclesiastical Province of the West Indies consists at present of eight Dioceses. Naming them in the order of their establishment, they are: (1) Jamaica and (2) Barbados, created in 1824; (3) Guiana and (4) Antigua, created in 1842; (5) Nassau, created in 1863; (6) Trinidad, created in 1872; (7) Windward Islands, created in 1879; and (8) British Honduras, separated from Jamaica in 1870 and fully organised in 1883. In attempting to give some clear impression both of the position and area of this Province, and also of the various efforts that the Church is there making, it will be best to speak first of our work on the mainland.

DIOCESE OF BRITISH HONDURAS.

In the extreme West of the Province we have the Diocese of British Honduras. This has its base in the British colony of that name, which is in central America, to the south of Mexico and Yucatan. British Honduras contains about 8,000 square miles, much of it being fertile country capable of maintaining, in days to come, a great population. Leaving this colony and travelling south-eastward, we find that, along 1,300 miles of coast-line, and over those regions of the interior that are accessible from the Caribbean Sea, and also on the Isthmus of Panama, the Bishop of British Honduras has the care of Missions already established, and the responsibility of establishing others, for the benefit of a widely-scattered population many of whom are members and adherents of the English Church. The efforts of Bishop Ormsby, since his appointment to British Honduras, have already achieved this result, among others, that whereas three years ago only four missionary clergymen of our Church were working in those regions, there are now eighteen.

There are over 2,000 communicants. Very great are the spiritual needs of the members of our own communion there as well as of others; and very remarkable is their readiness not only to receive our ministrations but also to help and support them. Bear in mind that this *first section* of the Province of the West Indies is on the mainland of Central America, and stretches over a coast-line of 1,500 miles.

VENEZUELA.

The next section of country on the mainland is Venezuela. The work needed here is similar to that which is being done in the outlying parts of the Diocese of Honduras :—namely the spiritual care of members of the English Church and others dwelling in those regions who desire our ministrations. This will be undertaken, in the first instance, by the Bishop of Trinidad, whose island Diocese lies just outside the mouth of the Orinoco. We should, in fact, have been able now to report the completion of plans for the regular carrying on of this work but for the recent political trouble between Great Britain and Venezuela. Of course there is nothing in our plans and purposes and methods of work which is of any political significance; but, all the same, our national and ecclesiastical authorities deemed it more prudent to let the political storm blow over before attempting to carry out those plans which had been agreed upon for organizing Missions of our Church in Venezuela. When these Missions are brought into active operation, they will constitute the *second section* of our work on the mainland, and will include a coast-line of about 1,000 miles.

DIOCESE OF GUIANA

The *third* and by far the most important section of the work which our Church is doing on the mainland is that which has its principal sphere in the great colony of British Guiana, while the missionary jurisdiction extends over Dutch and French Guiana as well. Thus the Province of the West Indies has its south-eastern termination at the Brazilian frontier; and at this point commences the missionary jurisdiction of the Bishop of the Falkland Islands, whose sphere of work extends round Cape Horn and as far as the Republic of Colombia on the Pacific. The Diocese of the Falkland Islands is not, as is sometimes stated, included in the West Indian Province; and indeed, if it had been so included, the immensity of the distances and the difficulty of transit would have prevented any connexion but one of a merely nominal kind. But recurring now to the Diocese of Guiana, let me mention a few facts which may help to show the results of past work. There are 45 clergy, 90 catechists, 100 day schools, 21,580 registered Church members. There is parochial work amongst the ordinary and settled colonial population of white, coloured, and black people who speak English : there are Chinese Missions on the west coast at Carmounie Creek, Skeldon, New Amsterdam, and Georgetown. There are three missionary clergy and several catechists working among the East Indians; and there are Missions to the aboriginal Indians and, in some instances, to the mixed population on the Corentyne, Berbice, Demerara, Essequibo, Pomeroon, Morucca, Wainii, Barima, Arooca, and Mataica Rivers. The outpost Mission district reaches the north-western frontier of Brazil. The ordinary parochial work is partly supported by voluntary gifts, but chiefly from public revenue; the Mission work is mainly supported by voluntary contributions, of which S.P.G. furnishes a large share.

The work of the Church in this Diocese has, in the minds of English Churchmen, been associated with the name of its first Bishop, who was also the first Primate of the West Indies, Dr. Austin, who died in Demerara soon after celebrating the jubilee of his episcopate there. With him there passed away the old order of things in Church and State, and his successor, Dr. Swaby, has to face many, great, and unforeseen difficulties, including those which result from the failure of the sugar industry, and from the consequent raising of the question how far it is necessary to withdraw those State resources which have hitherto contributed to the maintenance of the Church.

DIOCESE OF JAMAICA.

So far I have spoken of our work on the mainland; and I must now ask you to travel in thought back again 1,500 miles to Jamaica, which is a convenient starting point for describing the island work of the Province. Having for more than thirty years taken an active and responsible part in the affairs of the Church in Jamaica, and having for the last seventeen years been Bishop of the Diocese, I should have much to say in regard to it if time permitted. But I am trying now to give a summary account of the Church work in the Province, and therefore my references to Jamaica must be brief. Our island lies in the north-west of the Caribbean Sea; its area is 4,300 square miles, and over this space is scattered, more or less thinly, a population which numbers nearly three-quarters of a million. We have our great difficulties, agricultural, commercial, moral and religious. Few persons realise them more vividly than I do. But, notwithstanding, I am full of hope for the future of the country and the Church, provided that the agencies necessary to our progress can be maintained in full vigour. I repeat now what I stated in print two years ago :—' If some political or other cataclysm does not intervene, and if the influences, social, political, educational, and religious, now being brought to bear on the population are steadily maintained, our people will, in the not far distant future, become an intelligent, free, prosperous, and loyal community of some two or three millions. But political impatience and tinkering, and lack of steadfastness and energy and devotion on the part of the Church of Christ, may wreck these fair prospects.'

Our Church, having passed through the crisis of disestablishment and disendowment (with what anxiety and effort it is not for me here to tell), is now fully organized as a voluntary Church, with all the synodical and other machinery necessary to give practical effect to its united purposes; and we are nearly self-supporting. This includes the somewhat modest maintenance of the Bishop of the Diocese and the Assistant Bishop, and 102 clergy. We have also 150 catechists, whose work as such, so far as it is paid, is maintained out of the voluntary contributions of the Church. Many of these catechists are also masters of our Church schools, of which we have over 300, the maintenance whereof is largely dependent on Government grants awarded as the result of examination. We have a Theological College for the training of our clergy and a portion of our numerous lay workers; we have a Missionary Society, deriving support from every parish, for extending our home work and contributing to foreign Missions; and we have trained and sent to the West African Rio Pongas Mission two black men who are working there as missionaries, one of them having taken with him from Jamaica a wife who is also a true missionary. We have a branch of the Brotherhood of St. Andrew, working on the simple and effective methods of lay service adopted by that great organization, and also including the training and maintenance of lay evangelists and colporteurs; and we have a Deaconess Institution with six deaconesses and about fifteen subordinate workers (many of them trained nurses), ministering to the sick and the poor and helping to meet the spiritual needs, especially of women, of all classes. Our registered communicants are over 43,000. The contributions of our people for the purposes of the Church are about 30,000*l.* a year. This is largely drawn from the labouring classes and small settlers; though some among our educated and upper classes are willing and liberal supporters.

DIOCESE OF NASSAU.

The Diocese of Nassau is next to Jamaica among our island Dioceses. It includes the numerous smaller islands forming the Bahama group, the main body of which lies 300 miles north of Jamaica. The Diocese reaches up to the temperate zone, and stretches from the coast of Florida on the west to Turks Island on the south-east. A great difficulty in this Diocese is means of access to the various islands, and this difficulty of access, as well as the distance, cuts off the Diocese itself from any very active communication with the rest of the West Indian Province. We may well be thankful to know that its spiritual interests are so effectively cared for by its devoted Bishop and the self-denying clergy associated with him, and that it receives a good deal of sympathy and help from the Mother Church. The population of the Bahama group of islands is about 50,000. There are 22 clergy. In 1845 there were 84 communicants, now there are over 5,000.

ISLAND OF CUBA.

The large island of Cuba lies between the Bahama Islands and Jamaica. It has hitherto been under Spanish rule, and most of its inhabitants are at least nominally Roman Catholics. Some efforts for the benefit of the English-speaking people were begun some years ago under the auspices of the Bishop of Florida. There is need for these efforts as regards both the English settlers and also the natives around them, who dwell in great spiritual darkness. But the prolonged revolutionary struggle in Cuba has reduced everything to a state of chaos. As I passed, a few weeks ago, close along the east coast of the island, I could not help wondering how much of the news we hear from Cuba is true, and what is to be the end of the revolution. The pity is that, whether Spain or the revolution wins, there seems in either case no hope of a beneficial outcome of the struggle.

Republics of Haiti and San Domingo.

To the East of Jamaica and Cuba lies the island of Haiti or San Domingo. The western section of the island constitutes a republic of French-speaking black and coloured people. They are nominal Roman Catholics, but not much has been done in the way of elevating the people generally, either intellectually or morally. Besides several Missions carried on by British Noncomformist Christians, there is a Mission, led by Bishop Holly, from, or under the auspices of, the Protestant Episcopal Church of America; this work is important and necessary, but it has not always been adequately supported and maintained.

The eastern section of the island forms the Spanish Republic of San Domingo. The clergy of our Church in Turks Island (the most south-easterly portion of the Nassau Diocese) sometimes visit San Domingo to minister to the English settled there. But there is need for resources which would render systematic work possible.

Diocese of Antigua.

Further to the east is the large Spanish island of Porto Rico, and adjoining thereto the small one of Vieques, where there are congregations (of English and others) ministered to by clergymen of our Church under the episcopal oversight of the Bishop of Antigua, whose Diocese may be said to commence here. If only there were resources available, the work of our Church here, as in the other islands last mentioned, could be indefinitely extended, to the great benefit of the people.

The Diocese of Antigua includes also the episcopal oversight of fifteen of the smaller West Indian islands, Dutch and French, as well as English. In some of these islands the work needing to be done by our Church is only the teaching of, and ministering to, small groups of English-speaking people; in others there is responsibility for that large part of the population which is attached to the English Church. In the Diocese of Antigua there are 37 clergy, 44 lay readers, and 12,947 registered communicants. The greater part of the amount needed for the maintenance of the Church is derived from the voluntary gifts of the people, who contributed last year 8,245*l*. The remainder is chiefly provided by S.P.G,

One of the greatest financial difficulties before the Diocese is the finding of resources for meeting the cost of maintaining the Church and school buildings, always a heavy item in tropical countries, and specially so in this Diocese, where many of them are of wood, and are becoming dilapidated.

F

DIOCESE OF BARBADOS.

The Diocese of Barbados consists of the island of that name, renowned for its complete cultivation and crowded population. Within an area of 163 square miles there is a compact and busy community of 180,000 persons, and there are 47 churches, with 58 clergy, most of whom are maintained by the State. There are 10 lay readers. The communicants are 20,600. The island Legislature has long made liberal provision for maintaining religious and educational efforts for the general population. In some respects this island is in advance of other portions of the West Indies. If the sugar industry should fail, it is impossible to forecast the future of this colony and Church. If the sugar industry should recover a fair amount of prosperity, and the Church continue, as at present established, to receive an adequate amount of financial support from the resources of the State, the problems to be solved by the Bishop and clergy and their active lay co-workers will be chiefly those of a social and moral character common to all our West Indian communities.

Many years ago the Principal of Codrington College, Barbados, who afterwards became more widely known as Dr. Rawle, first Bishop of Trinidad, successfully advocated the commencement of efforts in the West Indian Church to take up missionary work in West Africa. The Rio Pongas Mission was started, and has been carried on with considerable success to the present time. A large part of the financial resources has been raised in Barbados and other West Indian Islands, the remainder being obtained in England by the help of the English committee. S.P.G. also has latterly granted a subsidy. Most of the clergy and catechists have been natives of the West Indies.

DIOCESE OF THE WINDWARD ISLANDS.

For the present, however, the Bishop of Barbados is familiarised and burdened with the ecclesiastical difficulties which have arisen out of the disestablishment of the Church in the Diocese of the Windward Islands, the care of which he has voluntarily undertaken. This Diocese now consists of the islands of St. Vincent, Grenada, the Grenadines, and St. Lucia. There are in the Diocese about 16 clergy and 24 catechists. There is great need for more clergy and other workers; but financial resources at present available are very limited. Without the help given by S.P.G. it would be impossible to maintain the work already existing.

The population of the Diocese is about 144,000, of whom 45,000 may be reckoned as Anglicans, and the remainder as Roman Catholics, Wesleyans, Presbyterians, Moravians, and Hindoos. The Roman Catholics are in a majority in Grenada, and in St. Lucia they constitute the bulk of the population.

DIOCESE OF TRINIDAD.

The Diocese of Trinidad, which includes the island of Tobago, has an area of 1,800 square miles. The population numbers about 220,000, of whom a large proportion in Trinidad are imported East Indian labourers. The Church-people are reckoned to be about 57,000. There are 50 churches and 20 school chapels, 25 clergy and 32 lay readers. The Church in Trinidad, although disestablished, has the financial advantage of receiving considerable contributions from the revenue of the island to aid in its maintenance, and this, with the voluntary offerings of the people and assistance from England, may enable the Bishop to carry out vigorously the plans which he has inaugurated for the extension of diocesan and Mission work.

In the Tobago section of the Diocese of Trinidad the Church is disestablished, with, I believe, no assistance continued from State revenues; and here the pressing question of the moment is how to make provision for maintaining the Church in parts already occupied.

Concluding Remarks.

1. If you have been able to follow this imperfect sketch, you will have realised that there are peculiar difficulties of organization and maintenance to be met by the Church in the West Indian Province. The Province includes a vast area, and there is a great variety and mixture of races and nationalities, and of forms of civil government. Some regions are thinly peopled; and to minister to the scattered populations which make up some of the large parish and mission districts of these tropical regions is laborious work which taxes physical endurance to the utmost. In other cases there are wide expanses of sea to be traversed, not only by the Bishop in his visits of superintendence, but often by the priest in performing the duties of his ordinary mission. And frequently the available means of transit in the longer journeys are such as involve circuitous routes; and even in the smaller distances the beating up to the eastward against a baffling trade wind, which is often strangely persistent day and night for long periods, introduces into the work an element of great uncertainty, delay, and expense.

2. There is a Diocesan Synod consisting of Bishop, clergy, and lay representatives in each diocese in the Province. The powers exercised by some of these synods are limited in accordance with the nature of the connexion of the Church with the State in such dioceses. There is a Provincial Synod consisting of the Bishops of the Province, the clergy and representative laity in each diocesan synod exercising practically the functions of a lower house of the Provincial Synod in respect of matters affecting each diocese. There is provision in the constitution for calling together the Bishops and representatives of the clergy and laity whenever, in view of the cost in time and money owing to distances and difficulties of travelling, this may be found possible.

3. Apart from the East Indian and Chinese labourers, the great bulk of our people are those, or the descendants of those, who obtained their freedom about sixty years ago; and the question which we have, as Churchmen, to ask ourselves is, how, with the material at our command, can we best do our share towards developing in these regions of the

earth orderly, progressive Christian communities? We should be unjust and ungrateful if we did not, in looking back over the past, exclaim in glad and thankful recognition, 'What hath God wrought!' The drawbacks are evident enough, but let us not forget the gains.

4. No account of Christian work in the West Indies could pretend to give even a complete outline of the subject unless it included a reference to what other bodies of Christians besides the Church of England have done, or are doing, in those regions. My present subject, however, is limited to a summary of the work of our Church.

5. With considerable differences of method, and under great variety of outward circumstances and surroundings, our Church is, I trust, everywhere maintaining a true and faithful witness for Christ, and labouring for the moral and spiritual elevation of the people, as well as seeking to promote their material progress. Notwithstanding many hindrances and many failures, we have manifold proofs that God is with us, and that our labour is not in vain in the Lord.

6. Since the last Lambeth Conference many of our standard-bearers have passed away, including Bishops Austin of Guiana, Rawle of Trinidad, Holme of Honduras, and Jackson and Branch of Antigua. Thank God that He has raised up others to take the places of these Bishops and carry on their work, in the persons of Bishops Swaby of Guiana, Hayes of Trinidad, and Ormsby of Honduras. Dr. Mather, I hope, will soon be consecrated for Antigua.

7. We need some of your most capable and best trained young English clergy as leaders. As regards Jamaica and some other portions of the West Indian Province, there is not much need for clergy from England of average attainments and powers, for most of the Missions can be supplied with men of this class born in the West Indies.

8. All our Dioceses are passing through a period of great financial difficulty, caused chiefly by the failure of our principal industry. In the earlier half of the century the Church Missionary Society helped largely in the missionary work of some West Indian Dioceses, and then handed over its Missions to the Diocesan Organisations. The Colonial and Continental Church Society has helped also to a certain extent, and schools have been assisted by the Christian Faith Society and the once vigorous Ladies' Missionary Society. But the main and most continuous assistance has come from S.P.G. and S.P.C.K. For some years to come this help will be specially needed in order to prevent the collapse of work on which so much labour has been expended in the past.

SUMMARY OF STATISTICS OF THE VARIOUS DIOCESES
OF THE PROVINCE OF THE WEST INDIES

The following summary is defective, but it is as complete as available information will permit; and the facts stated in this form may be useful to some persons desiring this kind of information.

THE MOST REV. THE LORD BISHOP OF JAMAICA 85

Diocese of Jamaica.

Churches 104 ; School Chapels and Mission Rooms 150 ; Registered Communicants 43,464 ; Clergy 102 ; Catechists 150 ; Voluntary Lay Readers 72 ; Sunday Schools 210, No. on books 30,472,. Average Attendance 16,459, Sunday School Teachers 1,696 ; Day Schools 309. No on Books 34,433, Average Attendance 19,085 ; Voluntary Contributions 30,000*l*.

Diocese of Barbados.

Churches 47 ; Church Members 20,600 ; Church accommodation 22,783 ; Clergy 58 ; Lay Readers 10 ; Baptisms 7,181 ; Confirmed 1,778 ; Marriages 1,030 ; Day Schools 150, Day Scholars 18,198 ; Sunday Schools 35, Attendance 3,295 ; Voluntary Contributions 5,620*l*.

Diocese of the Windward Islands.

Churches and School Chapels 31 ; Church Members 45,000 ; No. of Clergy 16 ; Lay Readers 24 ; Communicants 6,200 ; Marriages 275 ; Baptisms 1,900 ; Voluntary Contributions 3,622*l*.

Diocese of Trinidad.

Churches 50 ; School Chapels 20 ; Communicants 7,266 ; Clergy 26 ; Licensed Lay Readers 32 ; Sunday Schools 38, No. of Children on Registers 2,299, Average Attendance 1,387 ; Day Schools 43, No. of Children on Registers 4,759, Average Attendance 3,015 ; Baptisms 1,716 ; Amount of State Aid 3,900*l*. ; Sustentation Fund 1,140*l*.

Diocese of Guiana.

Churches and Mission Chapels 90 ; Clergy 44 ; Communicants registered 21,580 ; Children in Sunday Schools 5,998 ; Children in Day Schools 10,861 ; Services 24,387 ; Baptisms 3,714 ; Confirmations 1,790 ; Marriages 588 ; Offertories and Pew Rents $38,747.

Diocese of Antigua.

Churches 30 ; Registered Communicants 12,947 ; Clergy 37 ; Paid and Voluntary Lay Readers 44 ; Marriages 356 ; Baptisms 2,236 ; No. of names on Sunday School Registers 8,837 ; No. of names on Day School Registers 6,582 ; Amount raised for ordinary and special Church purposes 8,245*l*. 14*s*. 1*d*. ; Episcopal Endowment Fund 20,000*l*.

Diocese of Nassau.

Churches and Missions 96 ; Communicants 5,399 ; Clergy 23 ; Catechists (Honorary) 117 ; No. of names on Sunday School Registers 4,181 ; Sunday School Teachers 348 ; No. of names on Day School Books 1,629. Voluntary Contributions 2,380*l*.

Diocese of British Honduras. (*Including Central America.*)

Churches and Mission Stations 21 ; Smaller or sub-stations 27 ; Clergy 18 ; Lay Readers 22 ; Communicants 2,170 ; Children in Sunday Schools 990 ; Children in Day Schools 1,050.

THE RELATIONS OF THE ANGLICAN CHURCH TO THE CHURCHES OF THE EAST

BY THE RIGHT REV. G. F. P. BLYTH,
BISHOP IN JERUSALEM

It is with no little pleasure that I respond to-day to a request from your venerable Society that I should address you on 'The Relations of the Anglican Church to the Churches of the East.'

It is my privilege to represent our Communion at the mother-city of Christianity, where representatives of all other Churches have right of presence, without detriment to the episcopal jurisdiction of the Throne of St. James of Jerusalem ; just as their apostolic Founders had a common home at the Holy City. I represent there also the missionary character of our Communion, amongst those who certainly do feel that missionary spirit is the life of a Church, and whose own responsibility is primarily in the missionary enterprise of the Church of Christ in the East. This Society has therefore a right, which I gladly meet, to ask from me information on this subject. As the oldest distinctly Missionary Society, and the most appreciative of the Divine charge of the Bishops of Christ's Church, the Society touches the sympathies of all those who lead the Missions of the Church in foreign parts. And there is another aspect of the Society's aim, in the indirect missionary importance of which I am (jointly, I may say, with the Bishops of Gibraltar and in Northern Europe) much interested, having English chaplaincies to oversee in foreign parts ; I mean that aspect of her mission which regards ministrations to Europeans resident in the lands of other Churches. Some of these chaplaincies are of the first importance (witness your own at Constantinople) in bringing us into contact with our brethren of the East and West, and as setting before them our own method of fulfilment of the missionary commission of the Church.

In these few words of preface I have acknowledged the nature of the claim which I feel the Society has upon me. I have also stated the Catholic aspect of our representation at Jerusalem. But whilst I am saying that we of the Anglican Communion share the common right of the branches of the Catholic Church to episcopal representation at the mother-city of Christianity, both as an independent Apostolic Church and as a Missionary Church, I do not forget that the Throne of St. James has been more prompt than most of ourselves to acknowledge this. It was with true brotherly sympathy that the Patriarch of Jerusalem desired the revival of the Anglican Bishopric (in which he had had the concurrence of the Patriarchs of Antioch, Alexandria, and Constantinople), in order that our Communion might have representation at the Holy City. And the same prelate stated to me his appreciation and acceptance of the *missionary* character of our Church. I was speaking to him of what many

Anglican Churchmen feel a tender ground—the missionary work of our Church in the three Patriarchates of the East within whose jurisdiction I represent you. He said : 'The Missions of the Church of England, when not aggressive upon Christian Churches, and especially Missions amongst Jews, have my sympathy and my blessing : we are not now able to undertake them ourselves.' In these terms His Beatitude evidently reserved a missionary responsibility which the late Archbishop of Canterbury also acknowledged. And I think, too, he has (identically with the consequences of the Archbishop's words) forecast some future connection, which the Anglican Communion, in days of more intimate unity, may retain in Missions to the sons of Abraham, whether Jews or Arabs—a prospect of common responsibility and of brotherly association. The Archbishop's words are so true of the East, and so strongly to the point in considering 'the relations of the Anglican Church to the Churches of the East,' that they cannot be too widely understood. He said (I have but time to quote the leading words of an address of very great value) : 'The Eastern mind must be approached by Oriental Missionaries. The Apostles were Oriental Missionaries. Our only hope of influencing the world on that side is through the Oriental Churches. We must make the Oriental Churches what they once were. They are not a whit less clever than they were in the early ages of the Church. Everyone is aware of their intellectual subtlety, acuteness, penetration ; and their power of interpretation of Scripture is marvellous, and beyond our own. This is an underlying fact which must greatly influence the future. The Oriental Churches are the only Missioners who will produce an effect upon Mohammedans, and the problem is how to raise the Oriental Churches to the ambition of doing it. Let them rise to the cultivation and the knowledge of Scripture, which we seek, and to a certain extent obtain, and they will fall into their places directly. They are still, I am certain, Christ's great instrument for converting half the world.' I would add to the Archbishop's words the thought that Oriental Missions of the future (including surely the revival of the Missionary Church first planted, the Church of the Hebrews) may be very materially influenced by Anglican Church sympathy, experience, and co-operation. It is an unhappy and culpable misconception which undervalues the position and prospects of Oriental Churches, or which aggresses on them. They not only share with ourselves the eclipse which the unscriptural and unhistorical shadow of the Patriarchate of the West has cast over the Christian world, but they have to witness for Christ under an oppression which we ought not to forget. It was hard enough upon the English Church to wait for a *pallium* from Rome, during certain centuries ; but what would have been the condition of the English Church, in education, in knowledge of Scripture, in missionary activity, had the names of candidates for the Archbishopric of Canterbury, from the date of St. Augustine until now (for that about covers the duration of Church oppression in the Patriarchates at least of Jerusalem, Antioch, and Alexandria), to be referred to the Ruler of Islam, for the rejection of names favourable to the spiritual and educational growth of the Church, and had the Chair of Canterbury then been left too often to the ambition of the highest bidder? Those who remain what they are under existing circumstances, must have been preserved as by a miracle for some noble destiny presently to be revealed to them. It is due from us that we should be just to them; it is in our interest to desire their sisterly aid in advancing the cause of Christ. And over all is the constraining influence of His Will that there should be no severance, except by His excision, amongst the branches of the True Vine. The discords of Christianity are its chief hindrance in the East, but the Will of Christ is its unity. It is most touching to hear, as I commonly hear, prelates of the East speak of this Will of Christ, and say that with our back to our differences, and our face to the common Creed, we ought to pray for its fulfilment. Their expressions are not those of men who say sweet words which have no meaning. They are the grave plea of prelates of the sister Churches which have been in bondage for thirteen centuries, and they are addressed to a Communion which is spiritually free, and is become powerful throughout their older world, and in those newer colonies and Mission fields which have been opened to the world of to-day. They see *that* difference—and is it not for the free and the powerful to make the first move? But if there are real difficulties of action on their part, there are restraints placed also upon ourselves. The first thing that seems to strike an English mind with regard to the subject of intercommunion between Churches (though the shock is less prominent to the conservative Oriental) is, ' What a tremendous plunge it is !' Is it really so? Or is it that we want time and information for the entrance of a new and foreign idea? We cannot, of course, orientalise the West or occidentalise the East in ways of thought or liturgical habits. But our Lord did not found two Churches, but one Church. And the Church had one Creed. And let us ask what *formal* step was taken on either side, and when, to repudiate or excommunicate the other? We know communion is *suspended* between us; but does not suspension suppose a position which, having never been denied, requires only to be reaffirmed? I put that thought, only a few days since, to three prominent Bishops at Jerusalem, and they accepted it. There has been severance between the East and West, but that severance was the act of Rome. And we are not Rome. When did the Anglican Church take any formal action against the Oriental Churches? But there are other things to note also. A Patriarch of the Orthodox Church said to me (and we must remember that his *ecclesiastical* rank is equal to that of the Patriarch of Rome): 'I acknowledge the apostolic descent of the Orders of the Anglican Church, but I am somewhat doubtful about some of your baptisms. We require total immersion.' He admitted, however, that the validity of the Sacrament does not depend on quantity in the outward sign; and that there is not actual denial of the sufficiency of affusion, by the Orthodox Church. Upon this my Chaplain read to him the rubric of the Church of England, which prescribes total immersion, but accepts affusion, and does not recognize any other mode of administration. I told him that, of my own knowledge, total immersion was not infrequent, wherever asked for, in English Missions, especially in those of the Church Missionary Society, in the

East; and that I had myself lately immersed infants in some of these Missions. He replied, 'Then such Baptism is also valid.'

I can imagine one of my hearers saying, 'How is it that we hear so little of what goes on between our representatives in the East and our brethren of Eastern Churches?' Let me give an illustration, as briefly as may be, of the difficulty of publication of matters connected with those who are not free, as we are, but are tied by many restraints, political and ecclesiastical, and who naturally do not speak for the interviewer. Some years ago the Patriarch of Jerusalem gave permission to a distinguished American prelate, then a dean, and to our Canon Liddon to celebrate the Holy Eucharist in the Chapel of Abraham, in the Church of the Holy Sepulchre. He said: 'Yours is the only Church which has no representation here; but, because of various ecclesiastical and political difficulties, I can do but little to remedy that. But I can do this—I will allow to any Anglican priest who brings a recommendation from his Bishop occasional permission to use the Chapel of Abraham.' Of course this gives us no *footing* there, but merely a permission, which has since been renewed as frequently as desired. About three years ago we proposed to the Patriarch to be allowed to make certain repairs in the chapel, as a token of appreciation of this kindly act. This was cordially accepted. The plans were in every detail submitted to the Patriarch, and approved by him. The work was executed in Italy, and sent out to be fitted; and the occasion was one of much friendly feeling between us. But unfortunately, before the work was put in hand, a thoughtless English tourist, who held it nearly as bad as coquetting with Rome to use a Greek chapel, said scornfully, in the chapel itself: 'So, is this the *English chapel?*' The words were noted. And about the same time a correspondent of the *Church Times* wrote an innocently jubilant letter about the use of the chapel, in which he put forward the English occupation of it, not the fact that such use was a concession on each separate occasion. Both these stirred up the susceptibilities of a national Church of the Greek Communion, whose Church papers said: 'Here are these English claiming a chapel as their own, while we who are in full communion with the Patriarchate have no such privilege.' And at Constantinople it was supposed that we were after the usual game of fighting politics with Church weapons. So tense is the feeling about rights in the Church of the Holy Sepulchre, that a great Ottoman statesman once declared, as a way of keeping Europe employed, 'We have only to remove the guard of soldiers from the Church of the Holy Sepulchre to produce half a dozen European wars.' The consequence was that we had to hand over our materials to be fitted by Greek workmen, not without disappointment on both sides. And there were other consequences more serious than that. There is, I need not say, no political ambition whatever in any matter of friendly intercourse between ourselves and other Churches; but as politics are so commonly pressed in the Holy Land after this fashion, it is difficult to persuade our neighbours that we are not mischievous, especially when we are so given to writing to the papers.

But such difficulties as these do not exist in dealing with individual national Churches of the Greek Communion, or exist only in a limited degree. And we may expect to find, at any time, that the most important movements may be inaugurated through these national Churches, and notably through the goodwill and intelligence of the powerful Church of Russia. At the same time we must not forget, and she will not wish us to forget, that the four Thrones of the East are the four Patriarchates ; and that these act in concert with each other in Church matters, and that *their* action is necessary.

A few words here on the subject of intercommunion are not foreign to the purpose of this paper. It has two aspects, one between ourselves and other Churches, and the other regarding intercommunion amongst Churches severed from each other. The act of intercommunion is, of course, a very serious question, which has to be carefully, theologically and prayerfully considered on both sides. But to many minds it is a sort of *bugbear*. Their thought of intercommunion is not associated with the sanctity of our Lord's Will, but with the horrors of sectarian prejudice. What is it, really, in its simplest form ? Well, if you go and reside in some village, say of Armenia, Syria, Russia, where there is no service of your own Church, though there is between yourselves and the people the difference between Orientals and Europeans, you see that ' God has made of *one blood* all nations of men to dwell on the face of the earth ; ' and you sympathise with them, and they with you, in the ties of a common humanity. And so in their religious life, you see the parish priest instructing his people faithfully, and they worshipping according to their orders, with sincerity as real as your own. Christ has given to all Churches His *one Creed*, and you feel the ties of a common Christianity. At last, perhaps, on some great festival, you think, ' This priest's apostolic descent is as valid as that of my own clergy, and his ministrations as duly authorized. Why should I be cut off from communicating with Christ's people, because I do not endorse all the specialities of an Oriental Church ?' You ask permission to communicate, say on Easter Day, and are permitted with readiness and sympathy. This was the line adopted by that great missionary Bishop French, when studying Arabic in an obscure village in Syria. Now this would be an act of private and unauthorized intercommunion. But the case would be different were you able to say : ' My Church and your Church acknowledge each other's Orders and administration of Christ's Sacraments, and are on terms of formal intercommunion ; I claim, therefore, the right, as an English Churchman, of communicating at your altar, under the present circumstances.' That act would be based on the rights of intercommunion of Churches, not on those of private Christian charity. Where is the terror of it ? It will have to come, as inevitably as have international travelling and telegraphy. Time fails me to do more than glance at intercommunion between Eastern Churches. But it is a happy thought that if we *can* presently enter into formal and authorised intercommunion with one of these sisters of the Catholic Church, our Church may have grace, of our common sisterhood, to bring together those who are severed less by theological differences (which time has made mere films) than by political, natural, or geographical rivalries. You will scarcely believe, until you examine the theological points, how near some of these severed Communions are to each other, except for pride.

I have said enough to convince you that there is a very fine and wide field open to us, under the commonest Christian charity, and within the present conditions of our intercourse with the East and West. And the aim of promoting Christ's Will is worthier the ambition of a pure and Apostolic Church than is the Pharisaism which stands apart from sister Churches, or would Anglicise them, were that possible. It is English isolation which misrepresents to itself the case, and strikes against obedience to the charge of Christ. It is very easy to say the Churches of the East are superstitious, ignorant, debased, idolatrous. They *are Oriental*, which is not always intelligible; and they are under thraldom, which is not always remembered. But I would ask one of those who hurl such vain prejudices against the Rock of Christs' Will, to show me a more learned, more spiritual-minded, more charitable, more enlightened Catholic Churchman of their own party, than was the late Patriarch Gerassimos of Jerusalem, on the side of intercommunion. I should feel honoured to meet him.

Let me give a practical finish to so tempting a subject. I have now been your representative Bishop for more than ten years at the mother-city of Christendom—long enough to be trusted, I hope, by many. I have heard a world of sentiment, *pro* and *con*, with regard to that side of my Bishopric which touches our intercourse with Churches episcopally represented there. I went out to the East with the Oxford protest tied to my feet, and very heavy it has been; and Oxford has as yet made no counter movement. I still wait for scholars and means, to enable me to meet the challenge of a late Patriarch: 'We have done all that social kindliness can do; it is time to essay something further.'

Why does this venerable Society make the natural and becoming request to hear me on these matters? Is there one present who will do what a dozen might do, were we at Keswick, rise up and proffer help in such a cause? I want scholars—Christian scholars; and they will want means.

ENGLISH CONGREGATIONS ON THE CONTINENT

BY THE LORD BISHOP OF GIBRALTAR

AT the Missionary Conference held here nine years ago by the Society for the Propagation of the Gospel in Foreign Parts, I gave an address by invitation of the Society on the subject of 'English Congregations on the Continent.' In that address I sketched the past history of these congregations. In the address which I have the privilege of delivering to-day on the same subject I shall restrict myself to their present character, position, and work. The most striking fact to be noticed regarding them is their great increase. In the early days after the Reformation, when our Church was called upon to make independent provision for the spiritual needs of her people abroad, the chaplaincies which she established were confined to a few British factories, regiments, and embassies. The Englishmen who at that time settled or travelled abroad were few in number. But since wars have become comparatively rare, and facilities for travelling have been multiplied, our countrymen visit the Continent in annually increasing numbers for recreation, pleasure, health, or business. Thousands every summer spread over the mountains of Switzerland and the lakes of Northern Italy. Thousands every winter flee from the fogs and cold winds of England to the sunny and picturesque shores of the Riviera. English merchants, traders, artisans, miners, governesses are resident in all parts of Europe. Groups of our countrymen collect wherever there is a demand for skilled labour and industry. British sailors throng every seaport. And wherever our countrymen find their way they are accompanied by their Church in her tender solicitude to supply their religious wants. Most of the chaplaincies established for this purpose are in the patronage of the Societies at home. The Society for the Propagation of the Gospel has now 210 chaplaincies on its list, 147 in actual working, and 63 for which the arrangements are uncertain. The Society was entrusted by its charter with the care of British factories beyond the seas, in addition to its colonial and missionary work. And as early as 1704 the British residents at Amsterdam and Moscow received help from it in the form of salary for the chaplains, and books both for the English residents and for the people of the country. But it was not until 1862 that this continental work was taken by the Society regularly in hand. The Colonial and Continental Church Society also renders helpful service in providing religious services for our countrymen abroad, having begun this part of its work in 1859. It has now on its list 40 permanent and winter chaplaincies, and 200 summer chaplaincies. Besides nominating clergy, the two Societies assist many of the less wealthy congregations by small pecuniary grants. The Society for the Propagation of the Gospel now makes grants to the amount of 600*l.* per annum, in addition to the yearly grant of 150*l.* to Constantinople. The season chaplaincies are supported by a fund that is chiefly maintained by the offerings of the congregation. The expenditure of this special fund during the year 1896 was 2,231*l.* 11*s.* 9*d.* The Society has other funds for the support of its work on the Continent, e.g. church building funds, loan funds, and endowment funds. The grants made by the Colonial and Continental Society in aid of its permanent chaplaincies on the Continent amount to 1,900*l.* The winter chaplains receive the offertories, after paying all local expenses, as remuneration. Most of the churches, which are now to be seen in all parts of the Continent, are vested in one or other of these two Societies. The Society for the Propagation of the Gospel has on its list 44 churches. The Colonial and Continental Church Society has 47, and also uses 33 belonging to other reformed communities, some being hired, and some kindly lent. Our churches have been erected at the cost of the congregations themselves, with aid, in some cases, from one or other of these two

Societies, or from the Society for the Promotion of Christian Knowledge. Here and there churches have been built by private individuals, such as St. Paul's Church, Malta ; Christ Church, Cannes ; the Church of the Holy Cross, Palermo ; All Saints' Church, Dresden ; All Saints' Church, Bordighera ; Christ Church, Baveno. Besides the chaplaincies which are in the patronage of the two Societies, there are a few others in the patronage of the Bishop of London, the Bishop of Gibraltar, private trustees, or the congregations themselves. But in whatever hands the property of the church or the patronage may rest, all chaplains before entering upon the duties of their office must have received a licence from the Bishop of London or from the Bishop of Gibraltar. The chaplaincies in Central and Northern Europe are under the jurisdiction of the Bishop of London, who at the present time is represented by his coadjutor, Bishop Wilkinson. The Bishop of Gibraltar has under his jurisdiction the chaplaincies in Southern Europe, in the islands, and also along the shores of the Mediterranean, Adriatic, and Black Seas. As railways increase and travelling is made quicker and more comfortable, the number of our countrymen who frequent the Continent will probably continue to grow ; and to meet their wants still further chaplaincies and churches will be required.

When the subject of continental chaplains is mentioned, the idea presented to the mind of many Englishmen is that of services conducted by chaplains changing from month to month for the benefit of tourists visiting the Swiss mountains or the Italian lakes. But our Church fulfils still more important work through chaplaincies of a less fluctuating nature. In numerous winter health resorts there are chaplaincies held permanently by earnest and able men, who take extreme pains to supply their people with hearty and reverential services, and with helpful sermons fitted both to interest and profit cultivated minds, and to deepen the spiritual life. The office of a chaplain at one of these health resorts involves much anxious work, and demands great tact and experience. If in his congregation are some who live only for amusement, there are probably others who are in ill health, or are in sorrow, or are watching sick and dying relatives. In his pastoral intercourse with these, a chaplain will find not a few waiting for the voice of sympathy, counsel, encouragement, and consolation. And for those whom the atmosphere of hotel life abroad tempts to drift into a course of idle amusement, a chaplain who has his heart in his work will take care to provide means of employing leisure profitably through books or lectures. But it is especially for communities of English people permently resident abroad in the great cities and in the centres of commerce, or in towns like Zurich, where there are numerous young Englishmen studying in the university, that chaplaincies are needed. Such communities are spread over Europe. Each one of them has its own special characteristics and individuality, its own particular history, its own occupations, interests, difficulties, and troubles. Travellers who visit any one of these places, unless they should spend a Sunday there and attend service in the English church, might not be aware that it was the seat of an English colony, living much as we live in England, retaining the same English usages, except so far as business may necessitate a change. At some places the settlement may consist of families who have resided there for many years, and bear names well known to all the inhabitants. Some members of these families may never have been to England, but like their parents and grandparents before them have lived on the spot from childhood. As I travel from place to place, these English colonies come into view like pictures in a kaleidoscope. Here and there I find a colony gradually decreasing in number, trade having passed into other hands, or the merchants having gone with their families to England, leaving their interests to be represented by agents, with whom they communicate by telegraph. Though individuals occasionally may fall away from their Church, either from having married into a foreign family, or from having drifted into careless ways, or for the want of a permanent chaplain to provide for their spiritual needs, and keep them true to their allegiance, yet as a general rule our countrymen in these places are attached to the Church of their fathers, and exert themselves to maintain the chaplaincies : and very important it is that they should be maintained ; for apart from the higher purposes which they fulfil in fostering the religious life of our people, they are the means of bringing them together once, at any rate, in the week, sustaining their interest in one another, strengthening the bonds which unite them in one body, and preventing them from becoming merged in the population around.

A great hindrance to our work is the smallness of our resources. We have no funds available for the support of the chaplaincies beyond the offertory and other voluntary contributions raised from season to season or from week to week, except in the case of a few places which receive small grants from the Societies at home. Until late years, chaplaincies were maintained at our embassies and legations, and in the chief mercantile towns where British Consuls resided, by aid of a small annual Parliamentary grant made through the Foreign Office. The only places at which the congregations now receive this grant are Athens, Constantinople, Copenhagen, Madrid, Vienna, Marseilles and Trieste, the last two being retained as having exceptional claims for help, because frequented by numerous British sailors. The congregations at all other places are now left dependent on their own resources, and at some of them, such as Buda Pesth, Bucharest, Smyrna, Milan, Turin, where the permanent English residents are scattered, few in number and of slender resources, they experience great difficulty in maintaining a chaplaincy. The stipends consequently which they can offer a chaplain for his ministerial labours are miserably small, and barely sufficient to maintain a livelihood, even should the utmost frugality be practised. When English travellers visit such places and attend public service, they ought not to criticise severely everything that may seem amiss. If there are blemishes, they may be sure that other eyes have seen them besides their own. It is easier to discover than it is to remedy defects. The spiritual needs of the small English colonies scattered over the Continent require that these chaplaincies should be maintained ; but in places where the income is less than that given to a curate in England, where there is neither society, nor climate, nor scenery to attract, where the field of duty is narrow and discouraging, and where a man finds himself cut off from his friends, from prospects of advancement, and from the interest of our Church's life at home, we cannot expect the chaplaincies to be filled by the best men whom our Church can produce, or that the music and other accessories of worship should have reached the level of efficiency attained by our churches in London.

A further hindrance on which I would say a word is the frequent changes both in the congregations and in the chaplains. At places such as Berlin, Constantinople, Paris, St. Petersburg, and other great cities in which the chief representatives of our country are merchants, the permanent element is large; but since the invention of steam and the telegraph this element has been greatly reduced. At the winter health resorts, though the owners of villas and not a few others return year after year, the congregations are subject to perpetual fluctuations, which are a great hindrance in the way of systematic and continuous work. At the opening of each new season helpers have to be enlisted, committees recast, choirs formed, the acquaintance of their congregations to be made by the chaplains, and most of the work organised anew.

The chaplains also are continually changing. Places I might mention where the English residents sorely complain of the repeated changes. No sooner have they become acquainted with the chaplain than he leaves them for work elsewhere. To the passing tourist it makes little or no difference whether the chaplain is or is not permanent, for they have their churches with their regular ministrations and means of grace elsewhere. Not so with the permanent residents; to these members of our Church the chaplain is their only pastor to whom they can go for counsel or comfort; and if his ministrations are to be effectual, they must have learned to look upon him as a friend who knows their special wants and circumstances, and takes a personal interest in their individual welfare. If he comes among them for one year or for one season only, in search of health, rest, or change, though he may faithfully perform the services on Sunday, yet possibly he may never make the acquaintance of all the residents, who may live at a distance from one another, and in places hard to find, and he may not even discover all the poorer members of his flock. No doubt our Church has suffered abroad, as she has often suffered at home, from men remaining at their posts after they have reached that time of life when bodily strength and mental power generally begin to wane, and when, from being wedded to their own long-practised ways and usages, they are averse to change, though change and improvement may be imperatively needed. But if our Church on the Continent has suffered from chaplains staying too long at their posts, she has suffered still more from chaplains not staying long enough.

There are persons who represent the existence of Anglican Bishops, clergy, congregations, and churches on the Continent as being an intrusion, and maintain that when we are abroad we should worship in the churches of the country in which we are sojourning. But such a course is impossible, unless we are willing to forego the sacraments and other privileges of public worship. If any one thinks that such is not the case, let him make the experiment of living on the Continent, and let him ask a priest of the Roman Church to administer the Holy Eucharist to him, or to baptize his child, or prepare one for Confirmation, and see what answer he would receive ; he would find that these rights and privileges are not granted to members of our communion, and that in order to receive them he must forsake the Church of his baptism. It should, moreover, be borne in mind that our chaplains have other pastoral duties to perform besides that of conducting public worship. There are children to be instructed, young people to be sheltered from evil, sick and dying to be visited, and in some places there is much work to be done for our sailors. The passing visitor sees nothing of this ministerial work, and yet it is most important work, and such as could never be transferred to the clergy of other communions, who, be it observed, might be Roman, Lutheran, Greek, Armenian, Coptic, according to the country in which our people might be settled. Until we are all united in one bond of truth and peace, and I must add, all speak the same language, our countrymen residing with their families abroad will continue to require English churches and chaplaincies, and as ours is an Episcopal Church, where she appoints clergy there for the sake of order and discipline, she appoints Bishops to superintend and supplement their ministrations.

But while we continue this work, I would notice that it is restricted to our own people. We have no mission to make proselytes or interfere in any way with other Churches. In accordance with the traditional policy of our Church, we confine our ministrations to members of our own communion. We maintain this attitude, however, in no spirit of insularity or selfish isolation. No ; we are ready to assist in all benevolent enterprises, wherever we are stationed ; we are willing to give counsel whenever we are asked for it, and to show sympathy whenever occasion offers. We are anxious, moreover, to further the cause of reform ; but we feel that the most effective and the most brotherly way open to us of furthering this object is to endeavour in our own services and ministrations to exhibit the principles, doctrines, and worship of a Church at once Reformed and Catholic.

All who are acquainted with the facts will allow that during late years our Church on the Continent has made good progress, and is well represented by her clergy. Speaking generally I can say, from personal knowledge, that recent years have been to us a time of earnest labour, life and growth. New and handsome churches, too numerous to name, have been built, and not a few existing churches have been reconstructed, enlarged, and improved. Among these there are some which would be objects of just pride to any English parish. In most chaplaincies, where there is not a church, there is a chapel or room set apart exclusively for religious services. It may be said without flattery that both chaplains and congregations have risen in most, if not in all our chaplaincies, to a higher appreciation of order and beauty as adjuncts of Divine worship. Nor should I forget to name the invaluable help which laymen have rendered, as members of committees at home and abroad, as churchwardens, as treasurers and secretaries, in managing the financial and other temporal affairs of the chaplaincies, in raising contributions for local and diocesan charities, in sustaining the fabric of the churches, and in discharging other kindred duties. In some places where the chaplains have changed every season, it has been due to them that the continuity of the work, the traditions, and the very existence of the chaplaincies have been maintained from year to year.

Fresh kinds of work also have been taken in hand. Within my own field of supervision, a diocesan Church-reading Union has been established with the view of promoting a definite and systematic study of Holy Scripture, the Prayer Book, Church history, and Christian literature. It has, moreover, been found possible to hold abroad and in London conferences of the chaplains and of lay representatives of the congregations for the purpose of considering subjects of interest—theological, doctrinal, and practical. Branches of the Girls' Friendly Society have been started in all the great continental cities for the purpose of helping young Englishwomen who may be studying languages, art, or music, or finding their livelihood as teachers, or servants in foreign households, or otherwise usefully employed. There are few places frequented by English residents where the Society is not represented now by associates. If zealously and wisely worked, this organization may render good service to the cause of religion and virtue by saving young Englishwomen, left in distant lands without the restraints, supports, and examples of their English homes, from sinking into evil ways, and by keeping them true to those habits of faith and piety which they learnt in early years. It is advisable that when such persons are going abroad alone they should be enrolled as members before they leave the country, and that they should be carefully commended to the associate of the place where they are to reside.

There remains one more field of pastoral labour for me to name, afforded by our sailors of the mercantile service, who in large numbers frequent foreign harbours. No class of our community more needs the ministrations of our Church, for no class is exposed to so many or so great temptations ; and yet no class till recent years has been more neglected. When I first entered upon my present office, I found that little effort had been made to promote their moral and religious welfare. No sailors' homes or institutes had been opened to protect them from the crimps and other agents of evil, who are ever on the alert to waylay our seamen as soon as they come ashore, and decoy them into wine shops, where they are drugged and sometimes robbed of all that they possess. Now, I am thankful to say, work is set on foot to aid British seamen in all the more important harbours within my own field of duty, from Bilbao, in the Bay of Biscay, to Odessa, in the Black Sea, through the agency of chaplains, lay helpers, and sailors' homes or reading rooms. If only sufficient funds can be raised year by year to maintain and extend the work, I hope to see all the larger foreign seaports connected by a chain or network of such institutions. There are two Societies of our Church, the Missions to Seamen and St. Andrew's Waterside Church Mission, which prosecute this work. But as the help given by these home organizations was altogether insufficient to supply our needs, and their aid had only extended to a very few ports, I was obliged to establish a special or Diocesan Society—the Gibraltar Mission to British and American Seamen. The work of this Mission is conducted for the most part in harbours where nothing had been done previously for the sailors, and elsewhere it cooperates heartily with the other societies which I have named, and supplements their work. The importance of the Mission is shown by the fact that about 135,000 British merchant seamen annually visit Gibraltar, 100,000 Malta, 36,000 Bilbao, 25,000 Genoa, Marseilles, and Lisbon, 10,000 Venice, Palermo, and Odessa. There is also much work to be done for our sailors in the ports of Central and Northern Europe, such as Antwerp, annually visited by 65,000, Rotterdam by 60,000, Hamburg by 57,000, Havre by 35,000, Dunkirk by 30,000, Boulogne by 27,000. In some of these ports, I am told, our Church has made good use of the opportunities offered by employing chaplains and lay helpers to visit the ships, by providing religious services ashore and afloat, and by maintaining seamen's institutes; but in many others the work, if done at all, has been done by undenominational societies, such as the British and Foreign Seamen's Society and the American Seamen's Friend.

The reports supplied by chaplains ministering to British seamen contain frequent complaints of the great obstacle to their work caused by the unnecessary increase of Sunday labour. Representations on this subject have been addressed to the principal shipowners and managing directors of steamship companies inviting their co-operation in discouraging and lessening, so far as possible, Sunday labour on board ships in port. Sir John Burns, the managing director of the Cunard Company, has recently given a noble example by issuing an order that no Cunard ship is to work in port on Sunday. This evil of Sunday labour has occupied the attention of the Missions to Seamen Society and its zealous secretary, Commander Dawson, R.N., who endeavour by representations made to the Government, as well as to the shipowners, to get Sunday cargo work and coaling in foreign ports restricted so far as possible, and to secure rest on the Lord's Day to British seamen.

One of the purposes for which the bishopric which I hold was established was to promote mutual knowledge and friendly relations between the Church of England and the historic Churches of the East. This purpose the four Bishops who have held the see have consistently and diligently endeavoured to fulfil. And owing in some measure to our efforts, and the efforts of the chaplains working with us at Athens, Corfu, Smyrna, Constantinople, Bucharest, and Odessa, many a cloud of ignorance, prejudice, and misconception has been rolled away, and brotherly respect and affection have been strengthened between ourselves and our Eastern brethren. We may think that the Churches of the East have been too stationary, too reluctant to admit change, too apt to centre their affections on the past. But whatever defects we find, or fancy we find, in these historic Churches, remembering the long and noble services they have rendered to the cause of Christ during long centuries of isolation, suffering, and bondage to Moslem oppression, we have scrupulously abstained from sowing seeds of discord or schism among their people.

Our congregations in many places contain a large American element. Americans have, indeed, churches of their own at Paris, Rome, Florence, Geneva, Dresden, and Nice, which are under the jurisdiction of the presiding Bishop, and are visited from time to time by a Bishop of their Church, deputed by the presiding Bishop to perform this duty. But in places where they have no churches of their own, they are accustomed to join in our services ; and in such cases a prayer for the President and for all who bear rule in the United States of America is said after the prayers for the Queen and the Royal Family of England. No pains, I believe, are spared to make Americans feel when they worship in our churches that they enjoy this advantage not as a matter of favour or courtesy, but as one of brotherhood and right. American candidates equally with English are presented at our Confirmations. American sailors equally with English are visited by our chaplains in foreign ports, and are admitted to our Sailors' Homes and Institutes. Except in places where Americans wish to have churches of their own, better, far better, that our worship should be a united worship Our language is the same, our faith is the same, our stated services, except in a few small details, are the same. By uniting in public worship we show to the world the Catholic character of the Anglican Communion. We deepen the sense of brotherhood ; we foster, strengthen, perpetuate that desire for peace and unity which now animates, and I trust may ever animate, the hearts of the two sister countries.

A few concluding words, let me say, on the important duty which belongs to English Churchmen on the Continent of making manifest and maintaining the true position of the Church of England. That position is unique. We are members of a Church which is both Catholic and Reformed. We have thus a twofold duty to perform. We have to maintain our character as bound to the Church of the earliest days by a succession of Apostolic order and a succession of Apostolic doctrine. We have also to maintain our character as a Church which three hundred years and more ago cleared herself of errors and abuses which the course of ages had gathered, and regained the liberty which she had lost. We must not, in our desire to advance projects of union, forget either of these duties. If our Church is ever to fulfil the hopes which have been built upon her, as being the only possible intermediary between the reformed and the unreformed Churches, and to be the instrument of healing the divisions of Christendom, she must be true and loyal to herself: while she shows goodwill to other communions, she must resolutely maintain her individuality, as a Church at once Reformed and Catholic, a Church which has cast off the yoke of mediæval error and bondage, has grown with the world's growth, and yet retains her links with the past, resting on the old foundation of Apostolic order, and grounding her teaching on the Holy Scriptures.

CONCLUDING WORDS OF THE PRESIDENT

THE CHAIRMAN concluded the meeting with the following words : —
The papers to which we have listened this afternoon have given us a picture of the various works done by the great Anglican Communion all over the world. We have had an account of the labours that Christians have undertaken in various parts, and the results of those labours, of the obstacles and hindrances that have been met with, and of the needs which they call upon us to help them to supply ; and I trust that all this will not be without its effect upon our minds. If it has no other effect immediately, let it at least have the effect of deepening the sense of unity by which Christians are bound to one another, and let us in our prayers constantly remember the great work which the Lord has given us to do, and which, according to the accounts we have received, the Church is now making an effort to fulfil.

His Grace then pronounced the Benediction, and the proceeding ended.

www.ingramcontent.com/pod-product-compliance
Lightning Source LLC
Chambersburg PA
CBHW020859160426
43192CB00007B/987